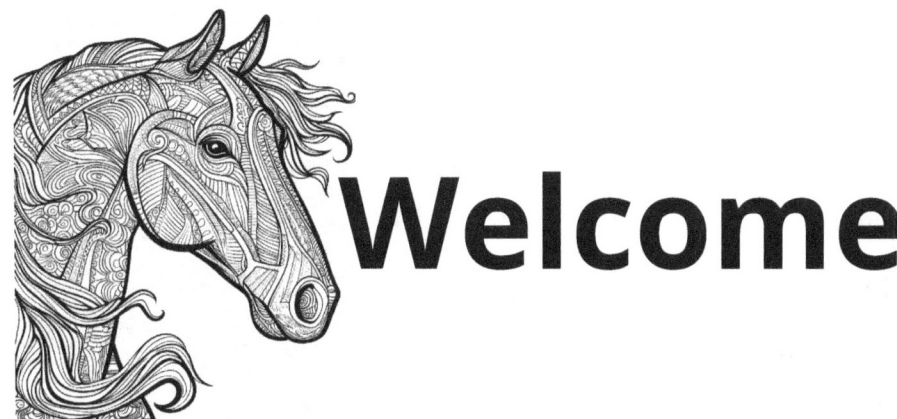 

Welcome

"67 Majestic Horses Coloring Book"!

Embark on a creative journey with each page, bringing to life the grace and power of 67 unique horses. Whether you're a budding artist or a seasoned equestrian lover, this collection invites you to explore your artistic side in the company of these magnificent creatures. Dive into a world where color and imagination meet the majestic beauty of horses. Happy coloring!

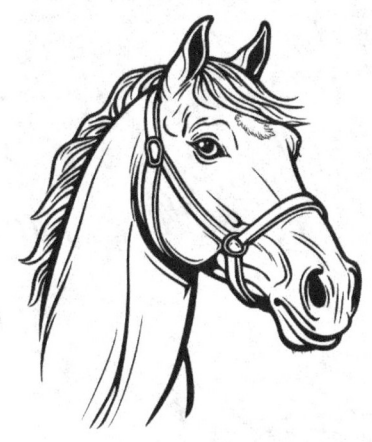 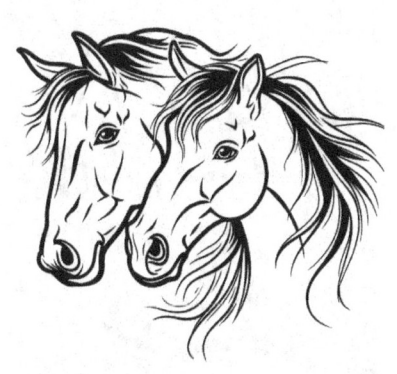

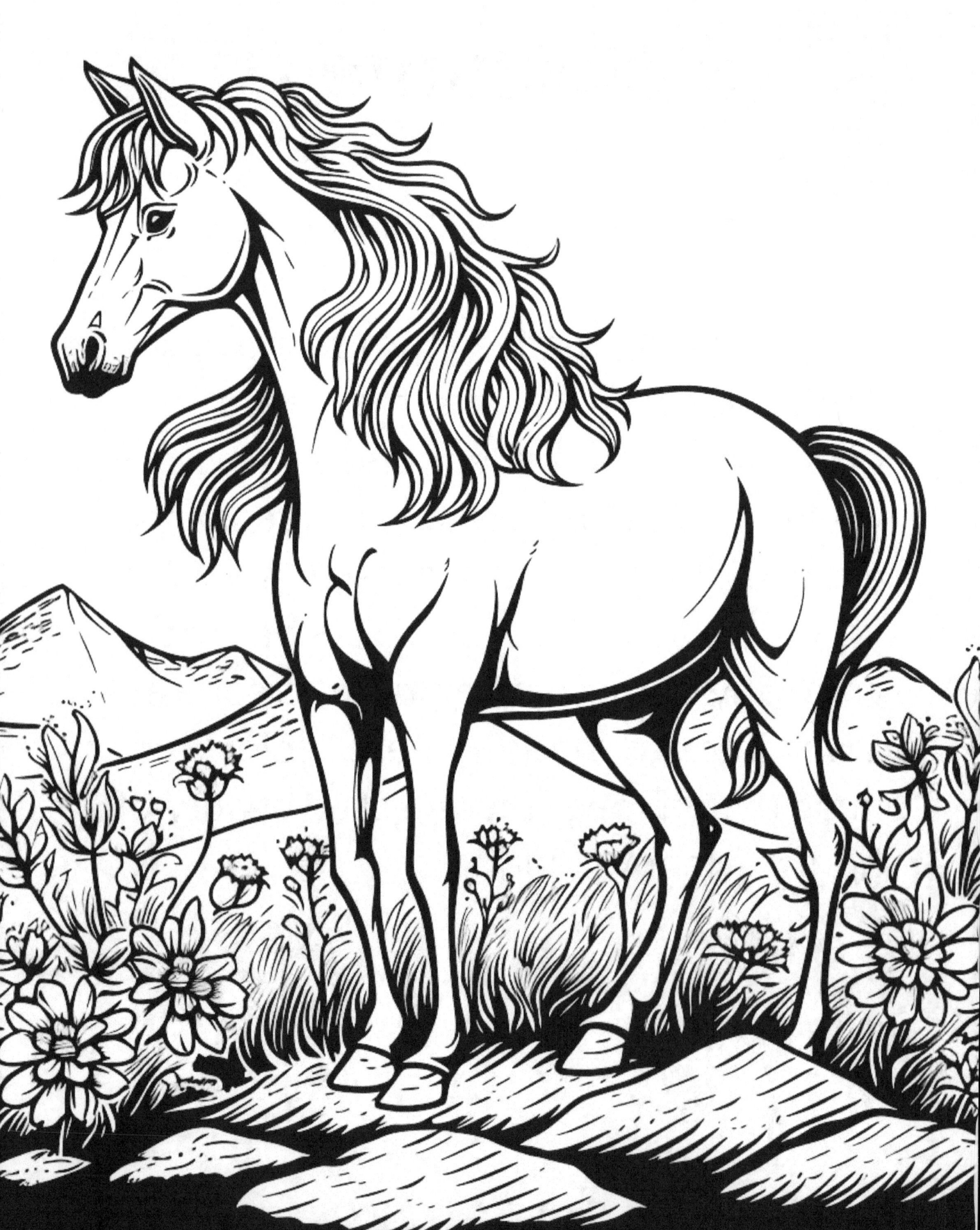

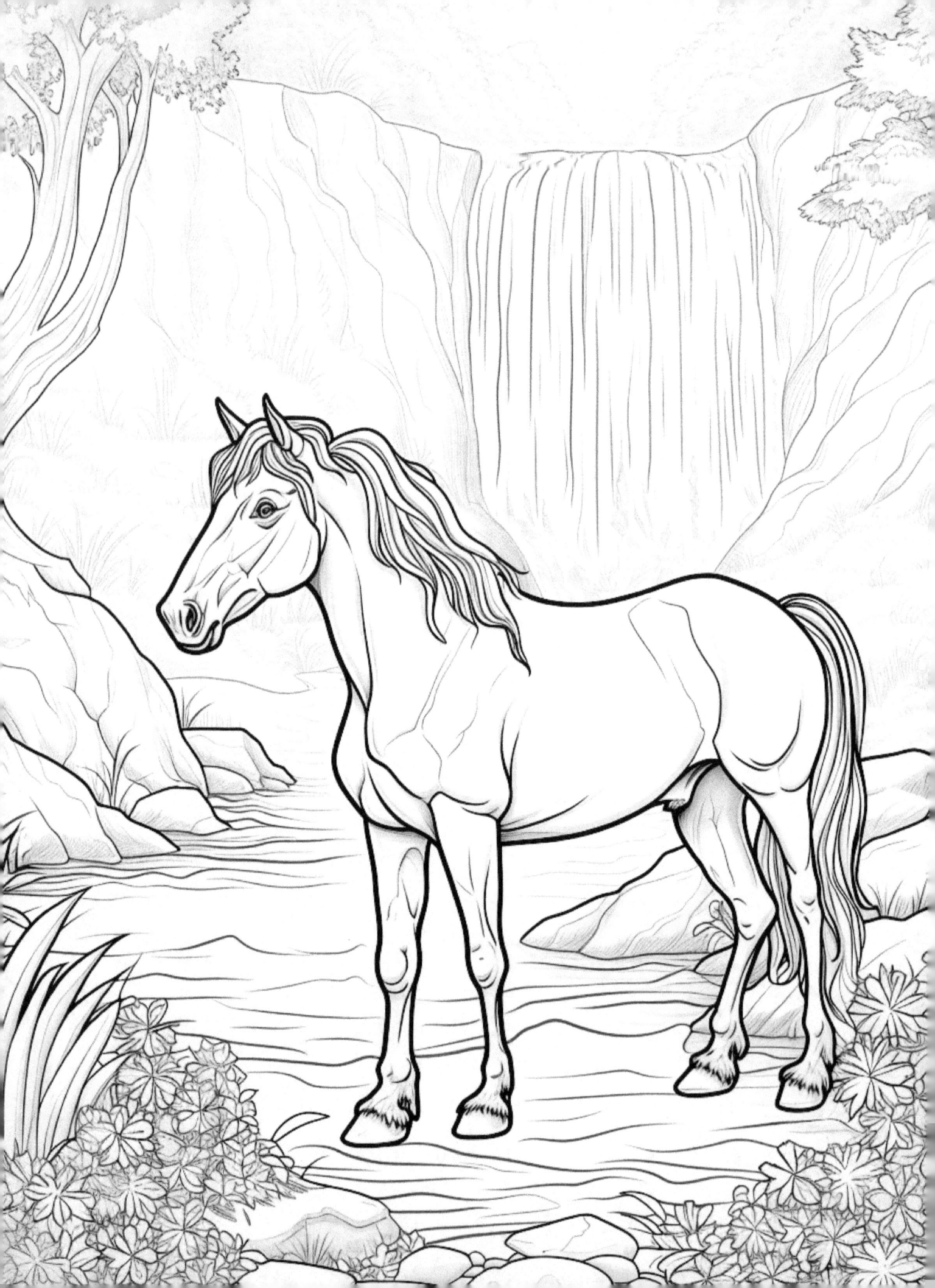

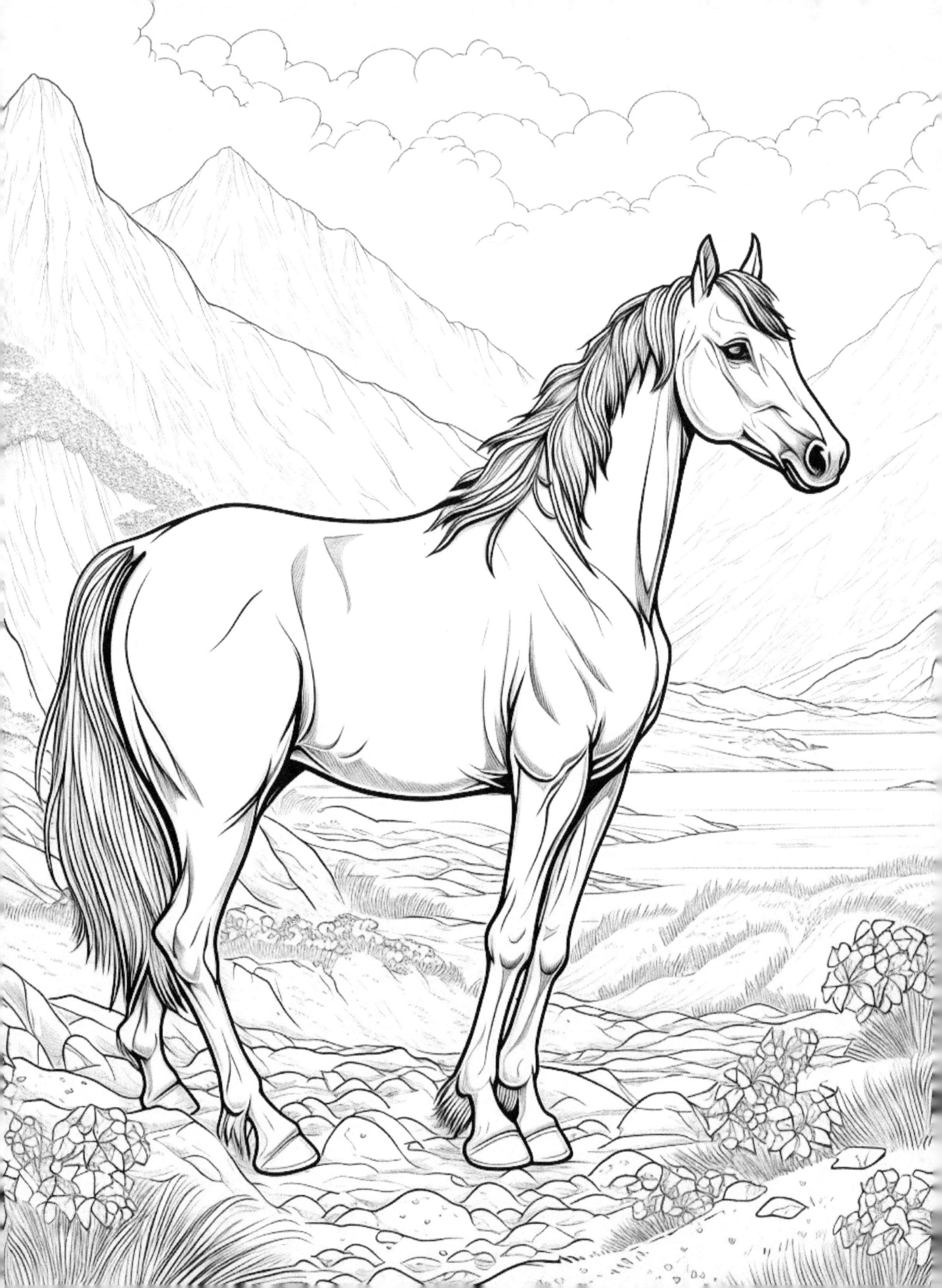

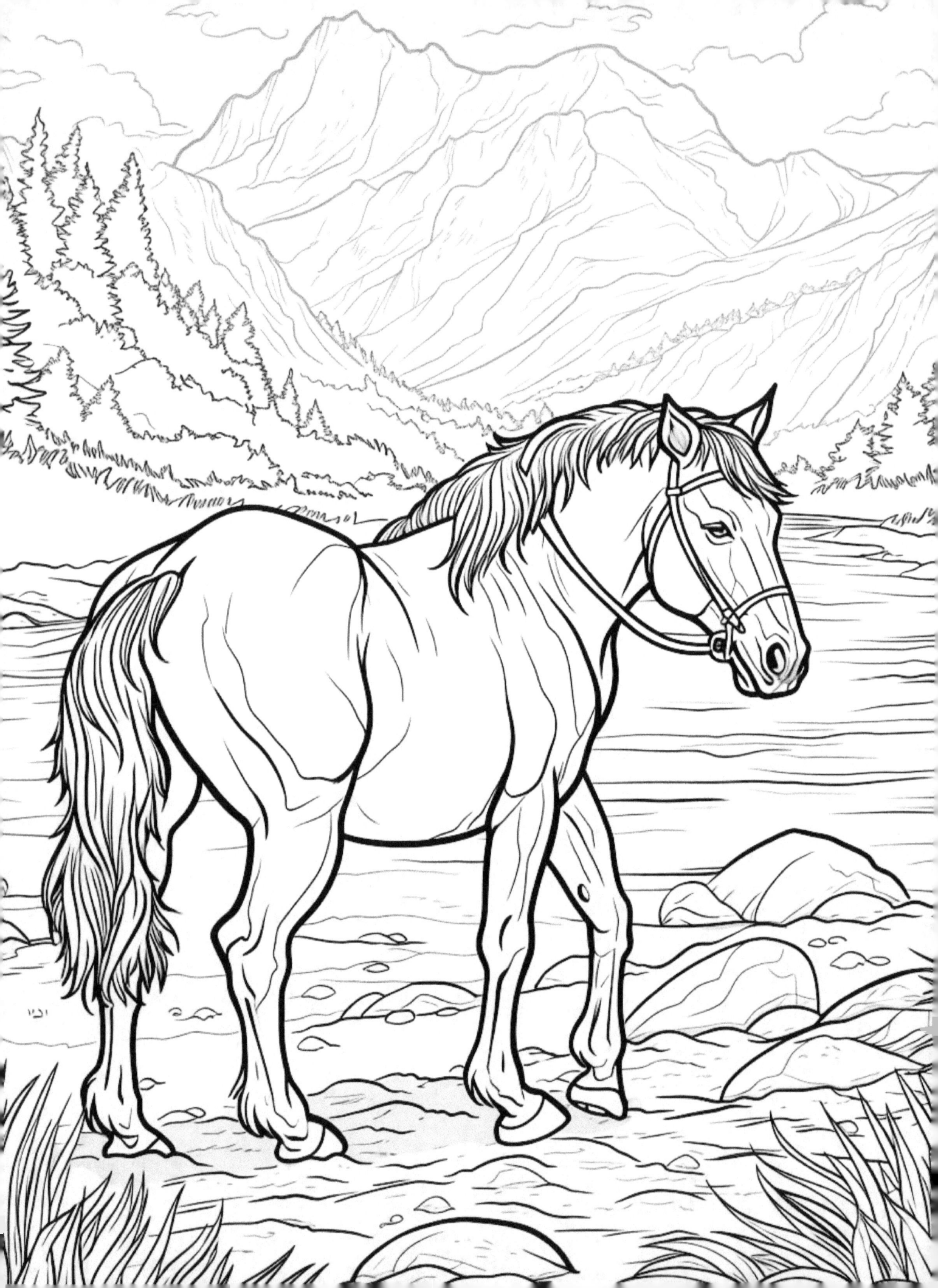

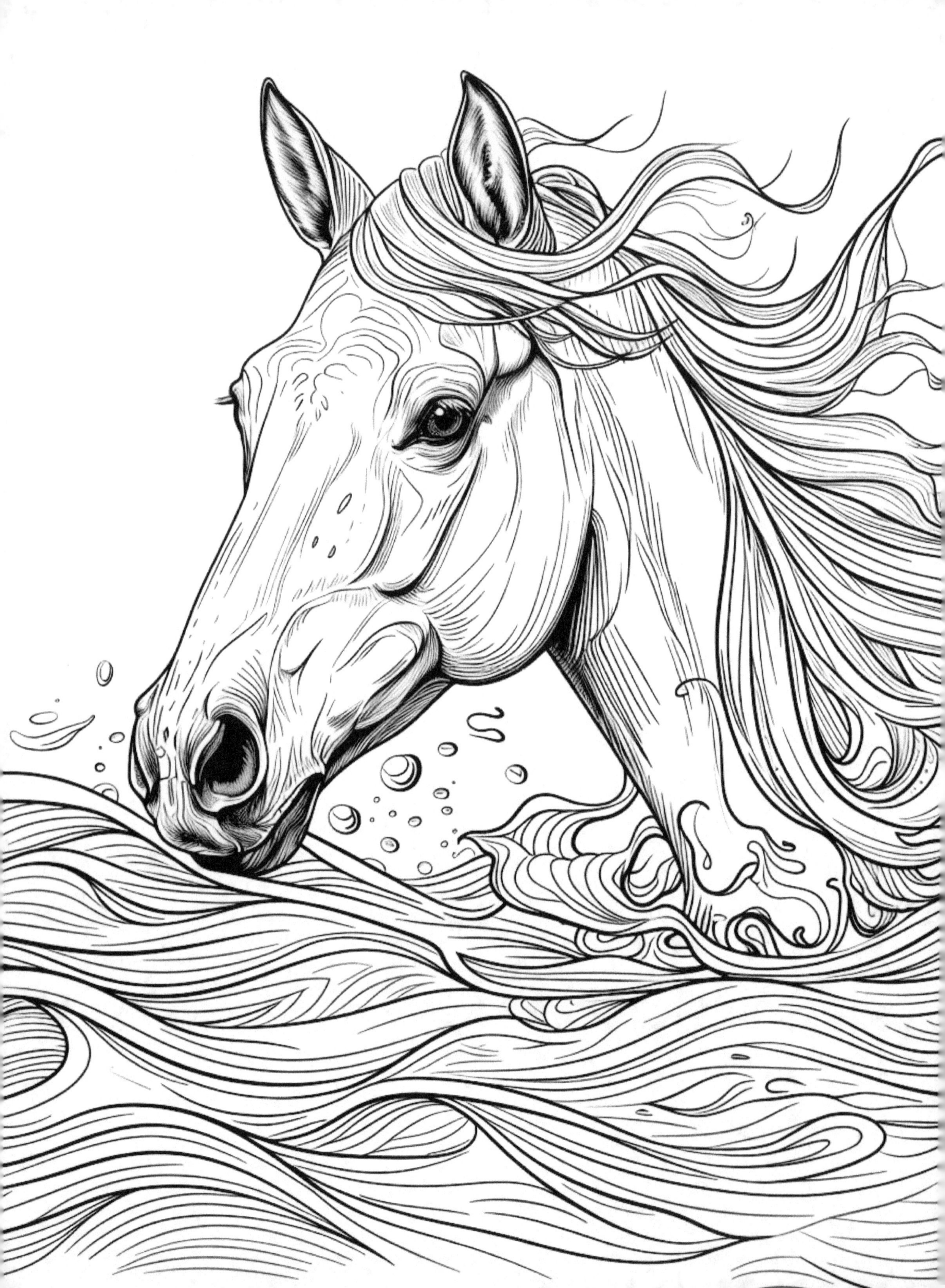

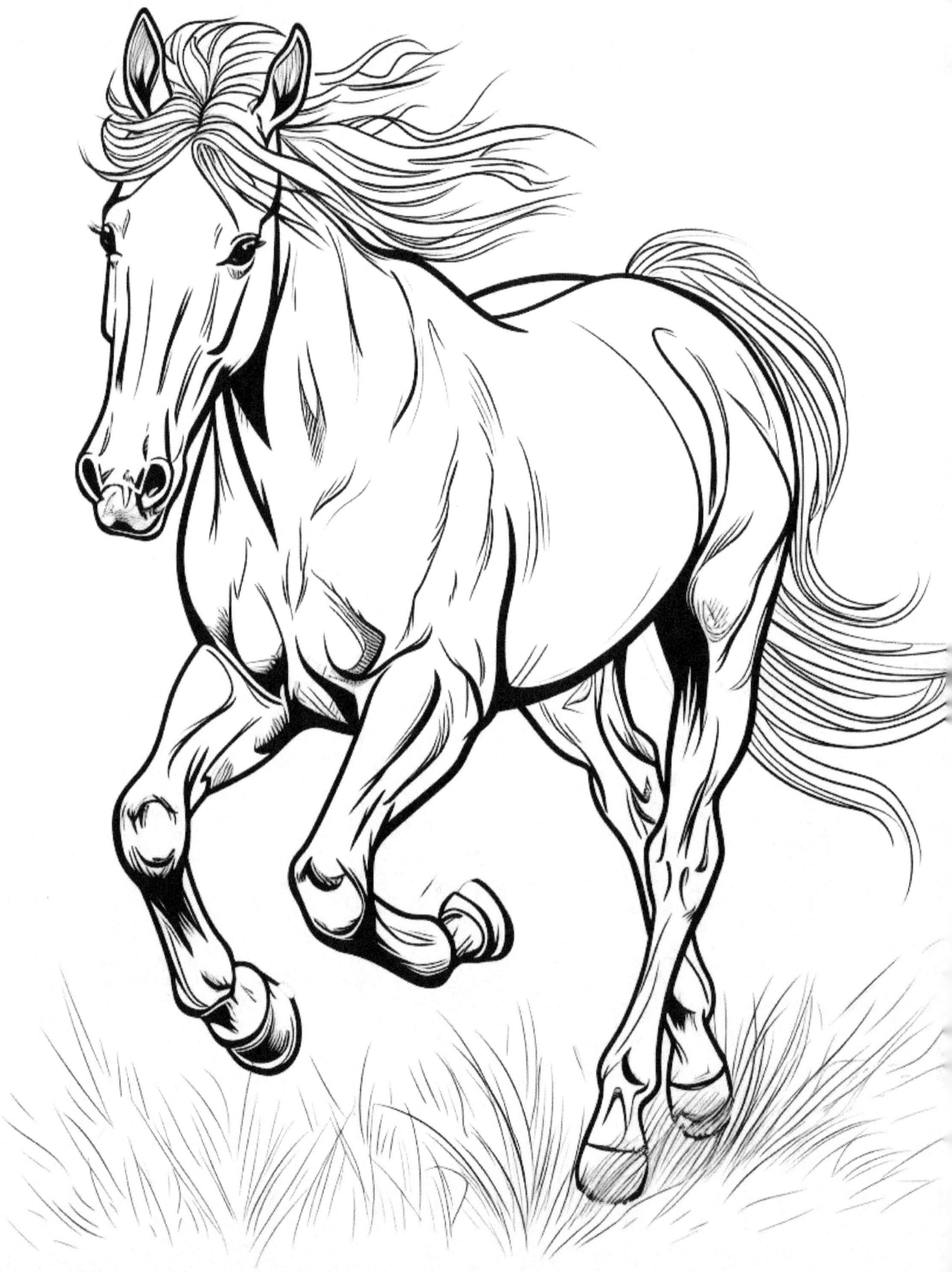

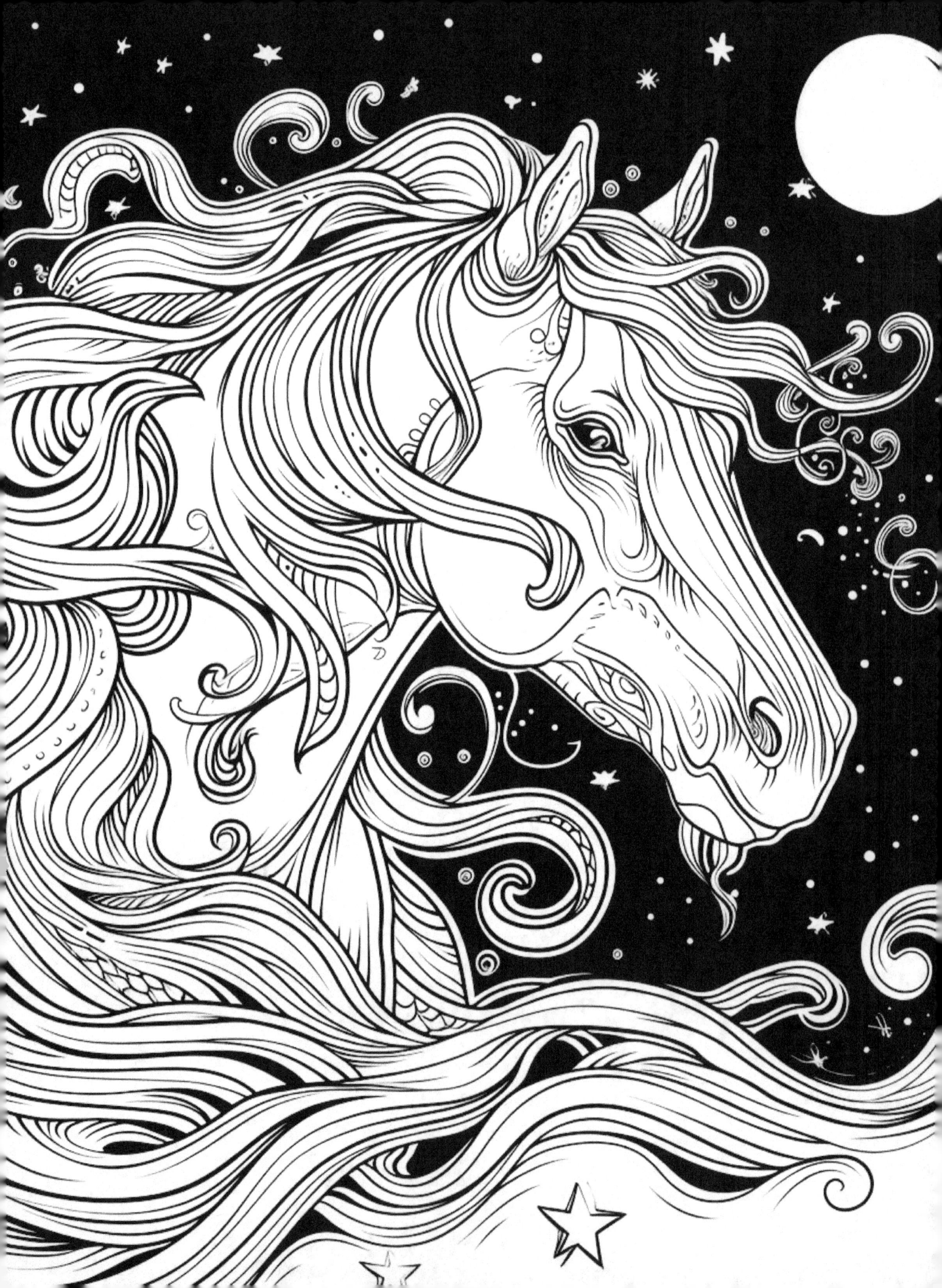

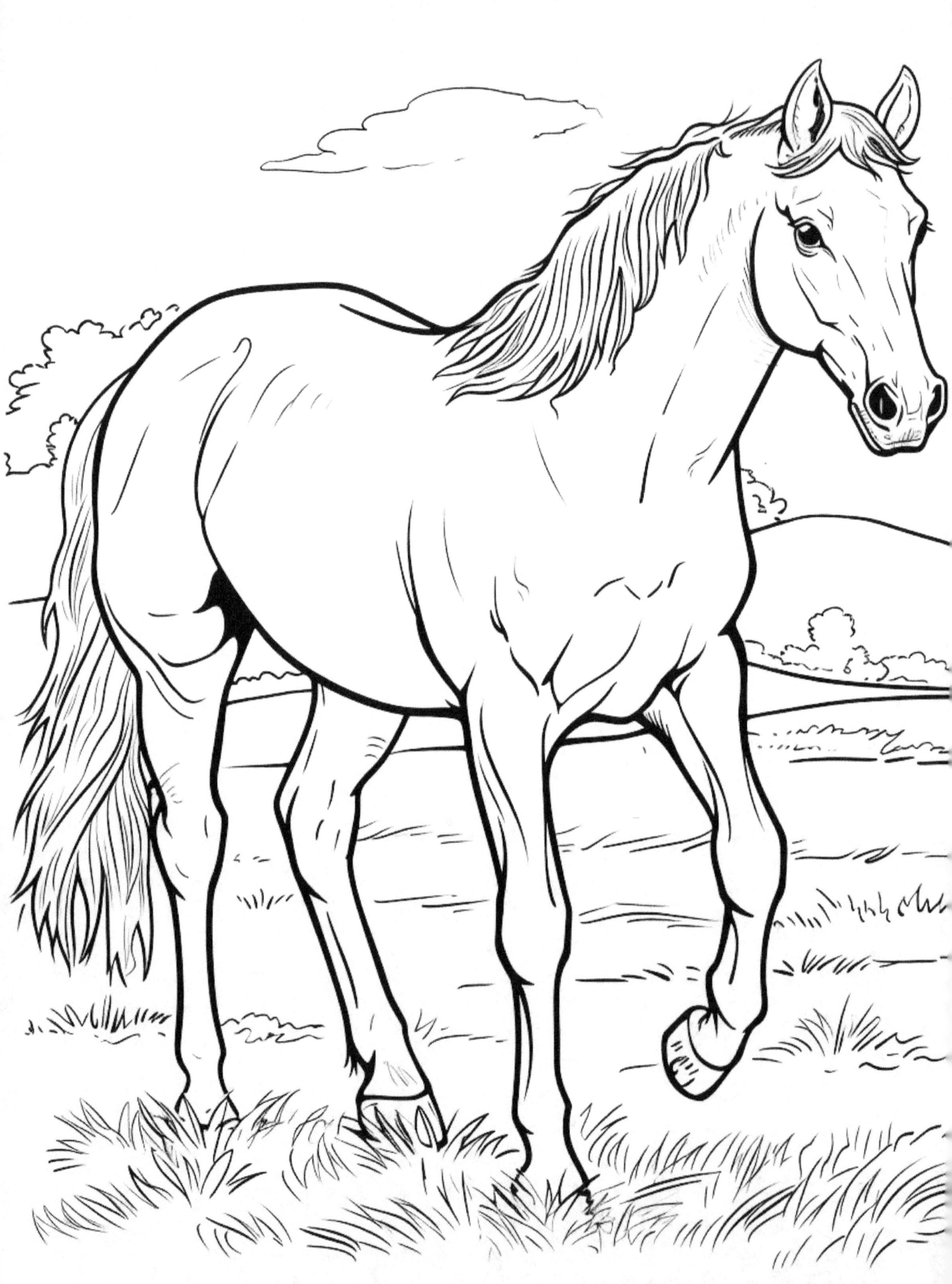

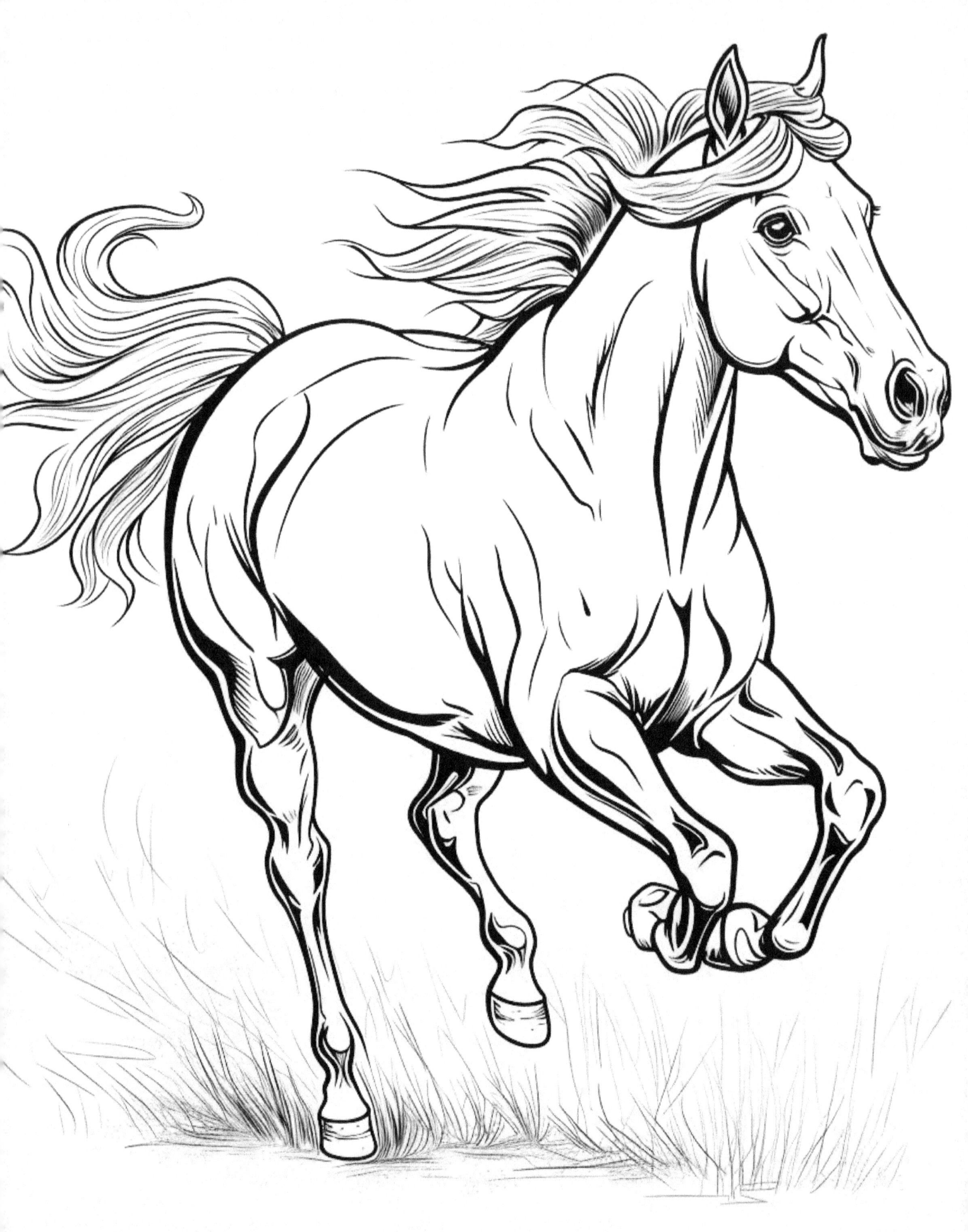

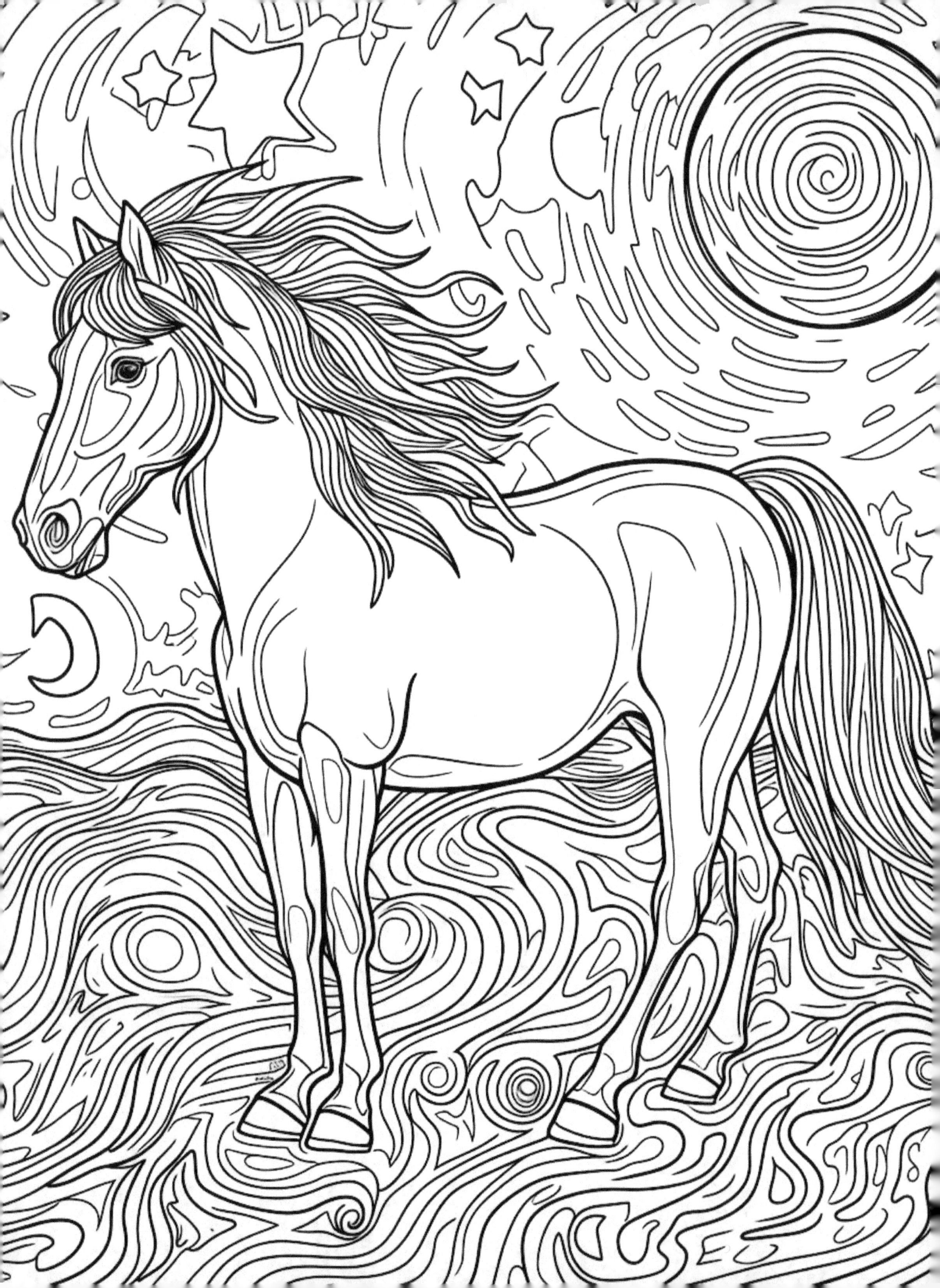

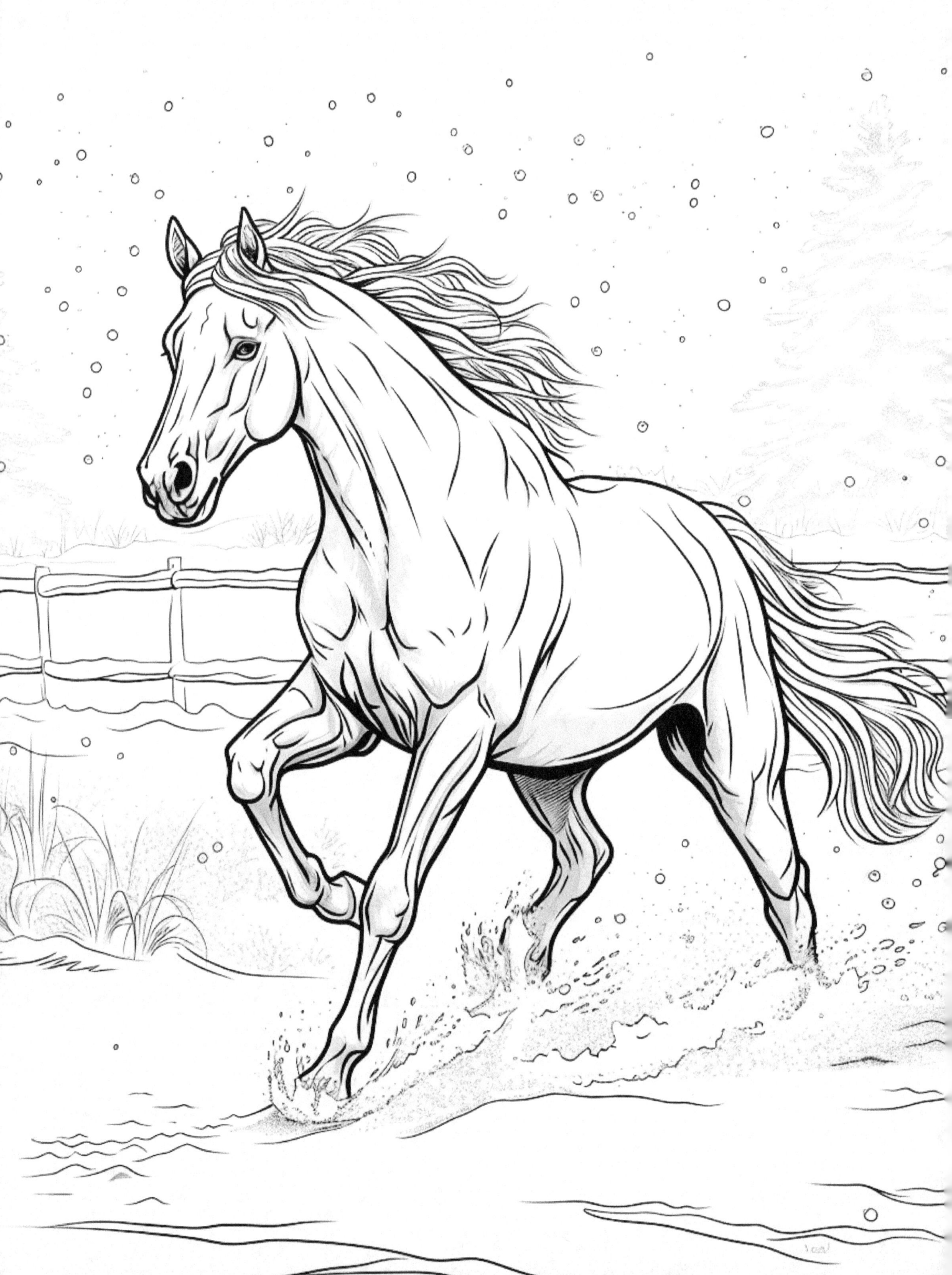

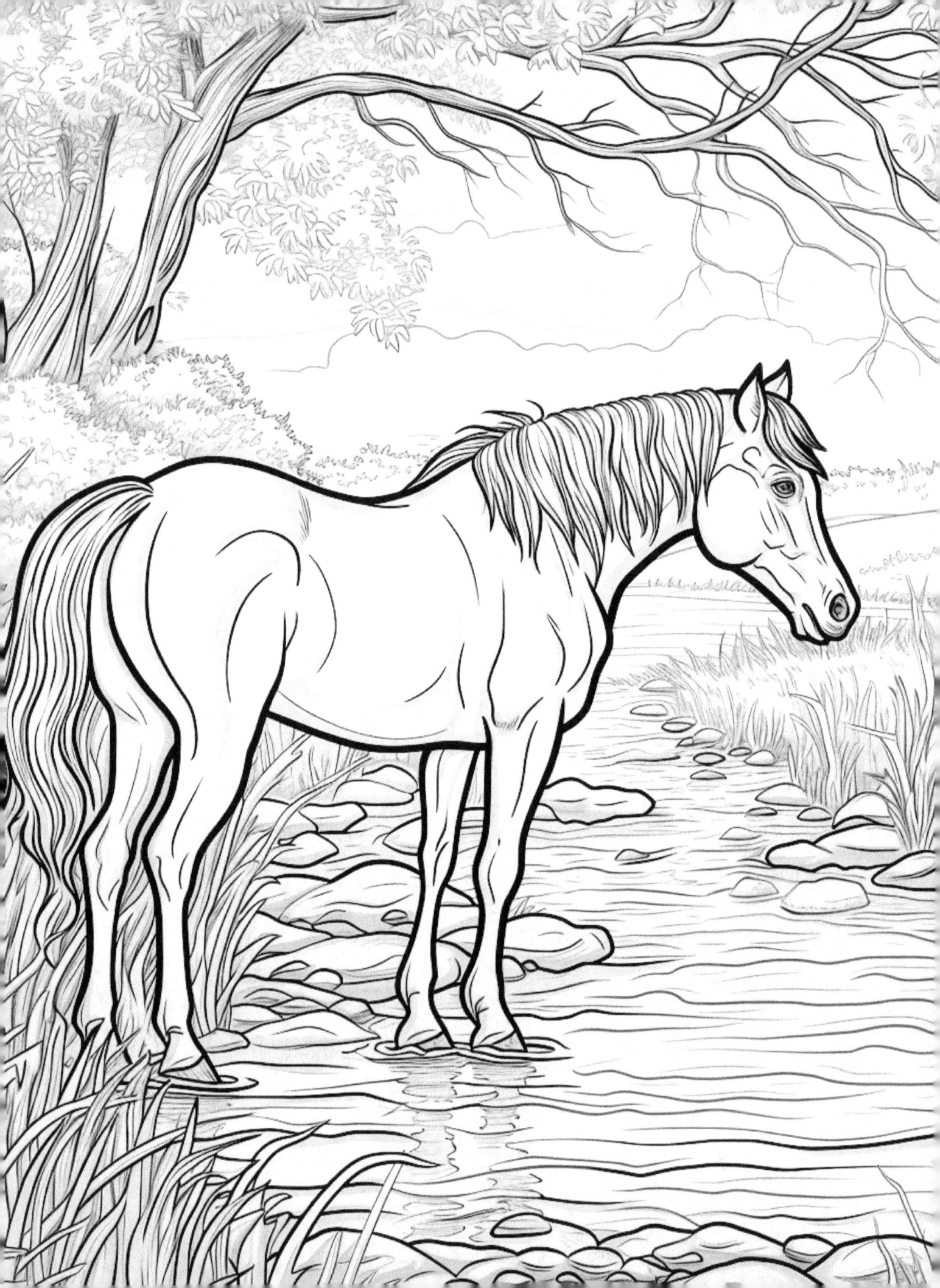

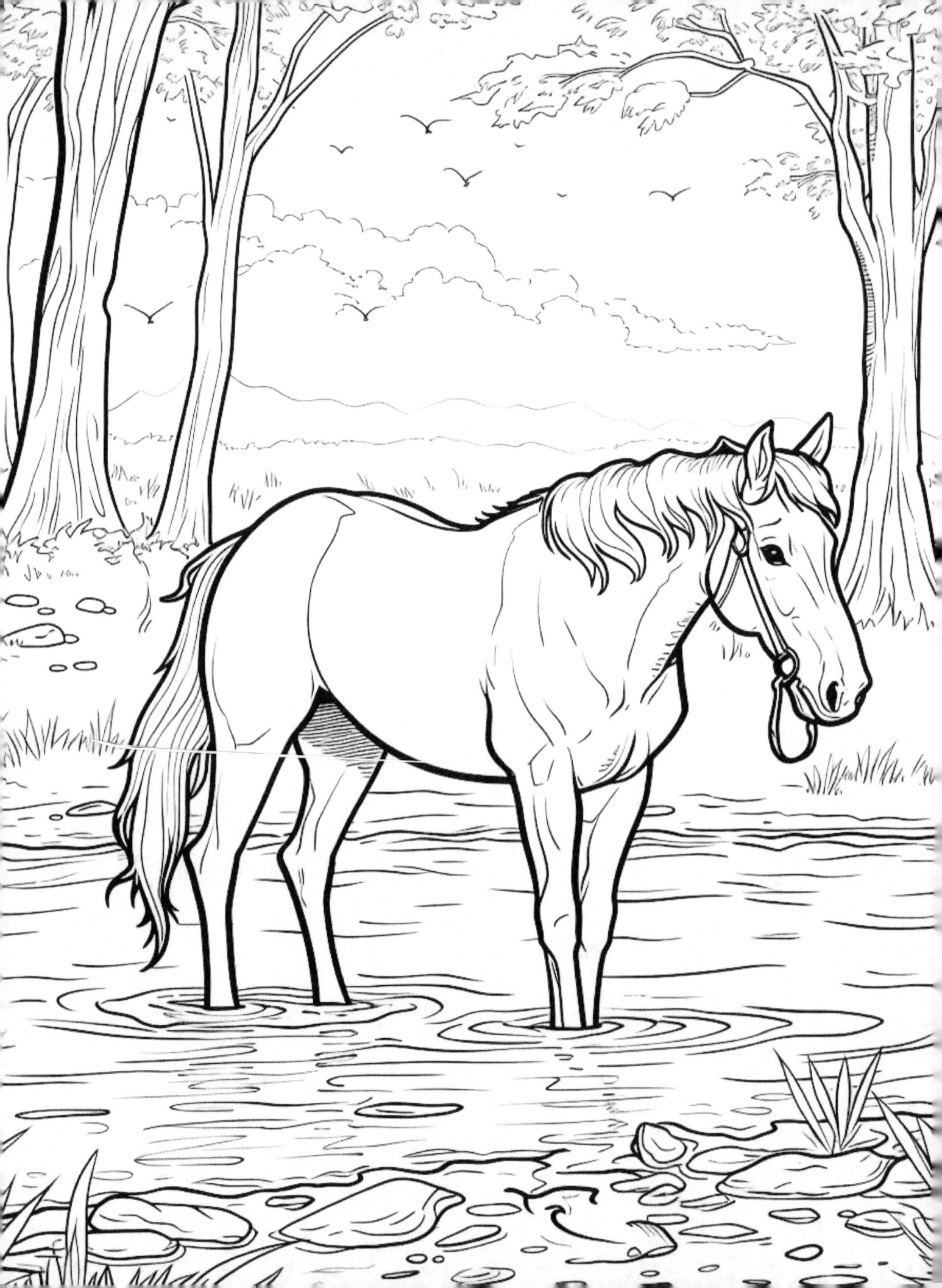

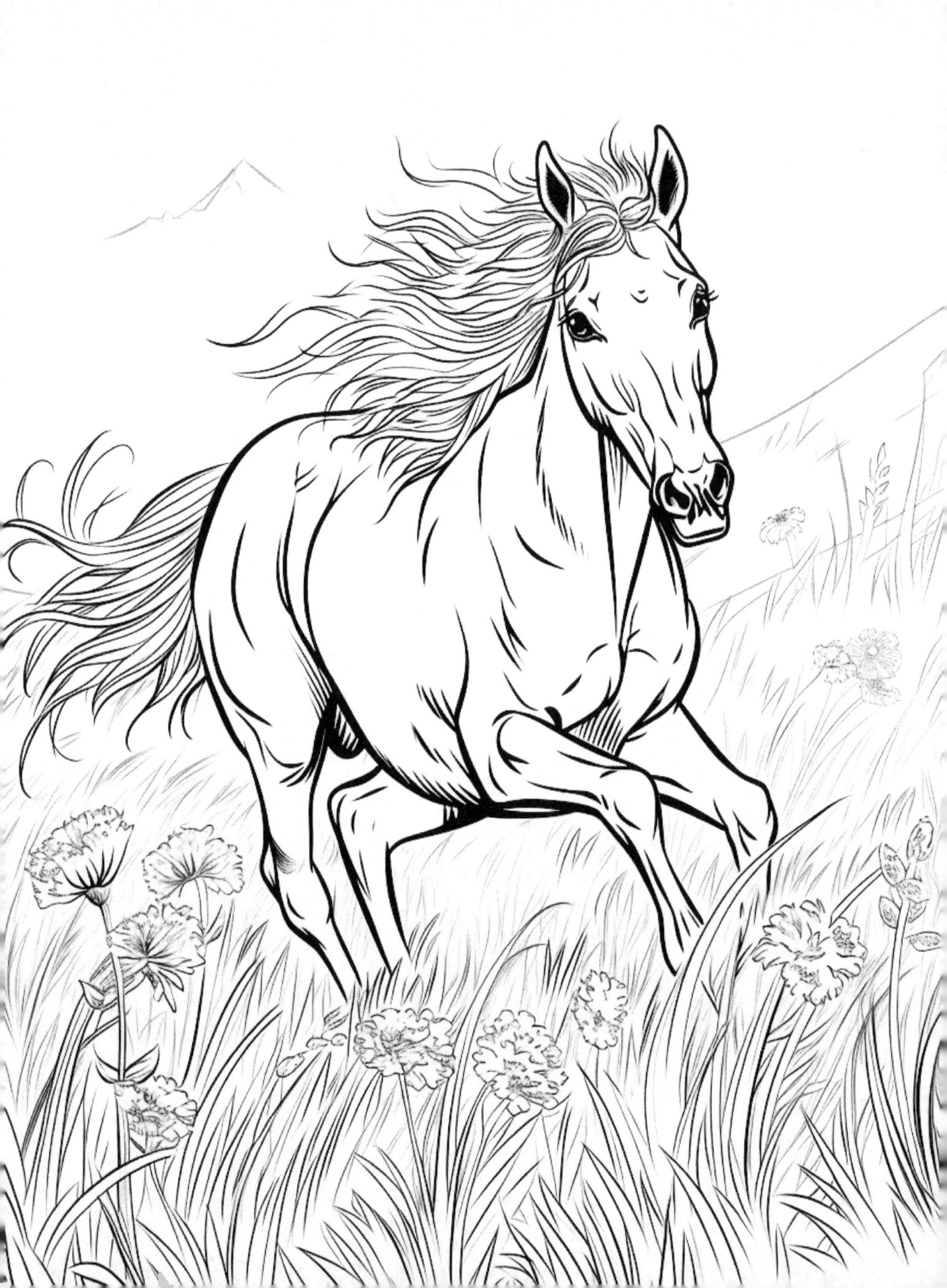

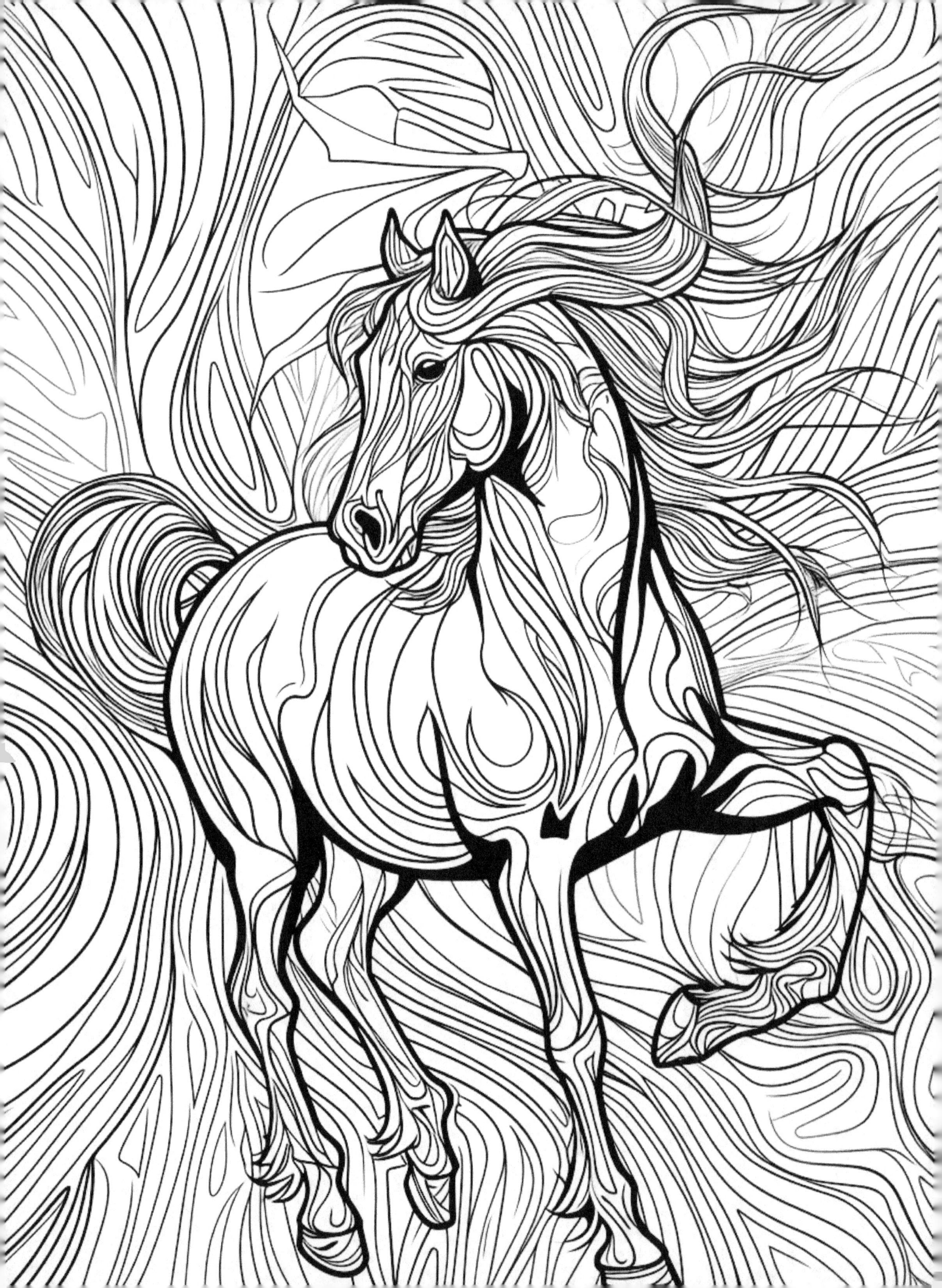

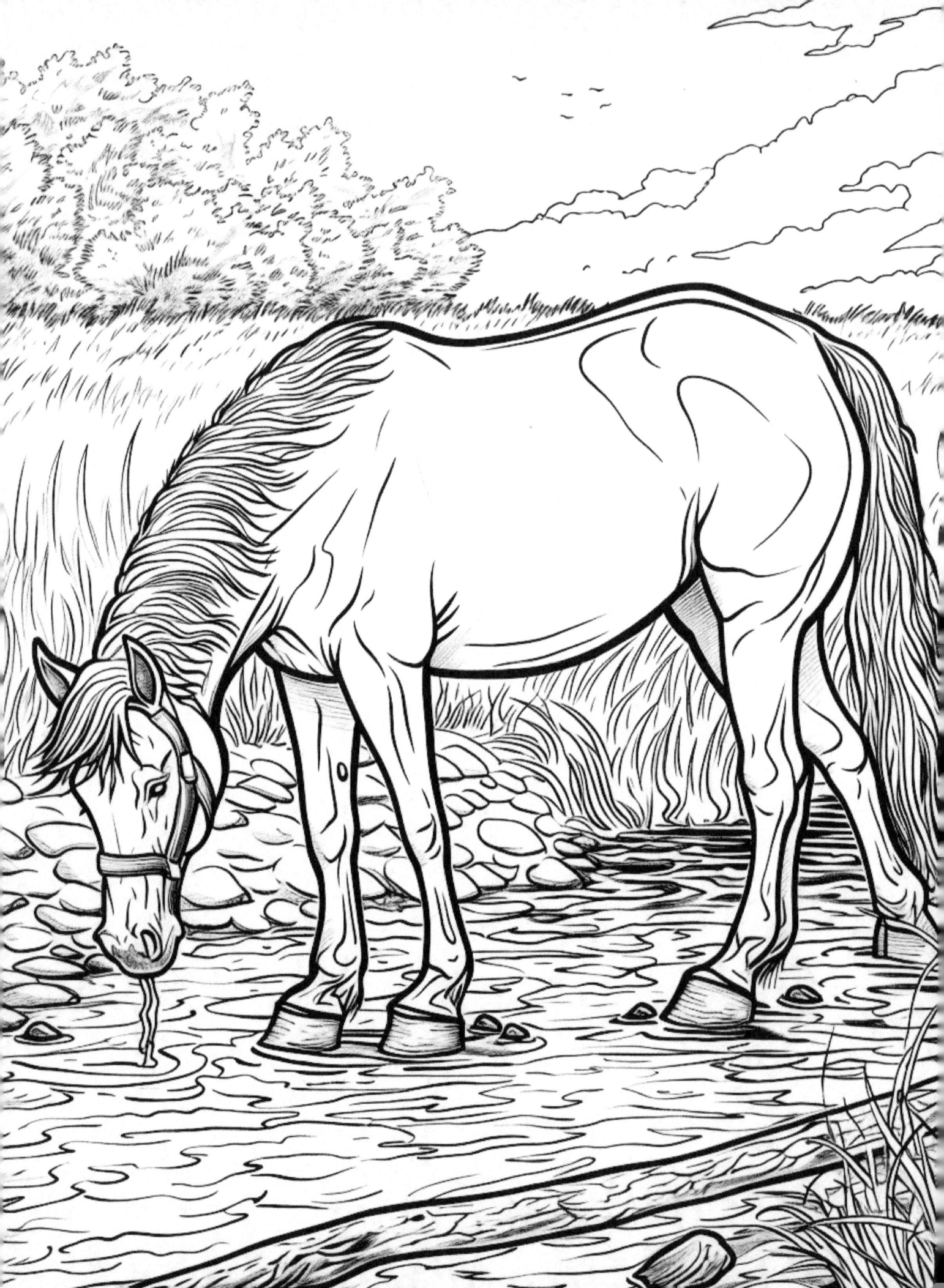

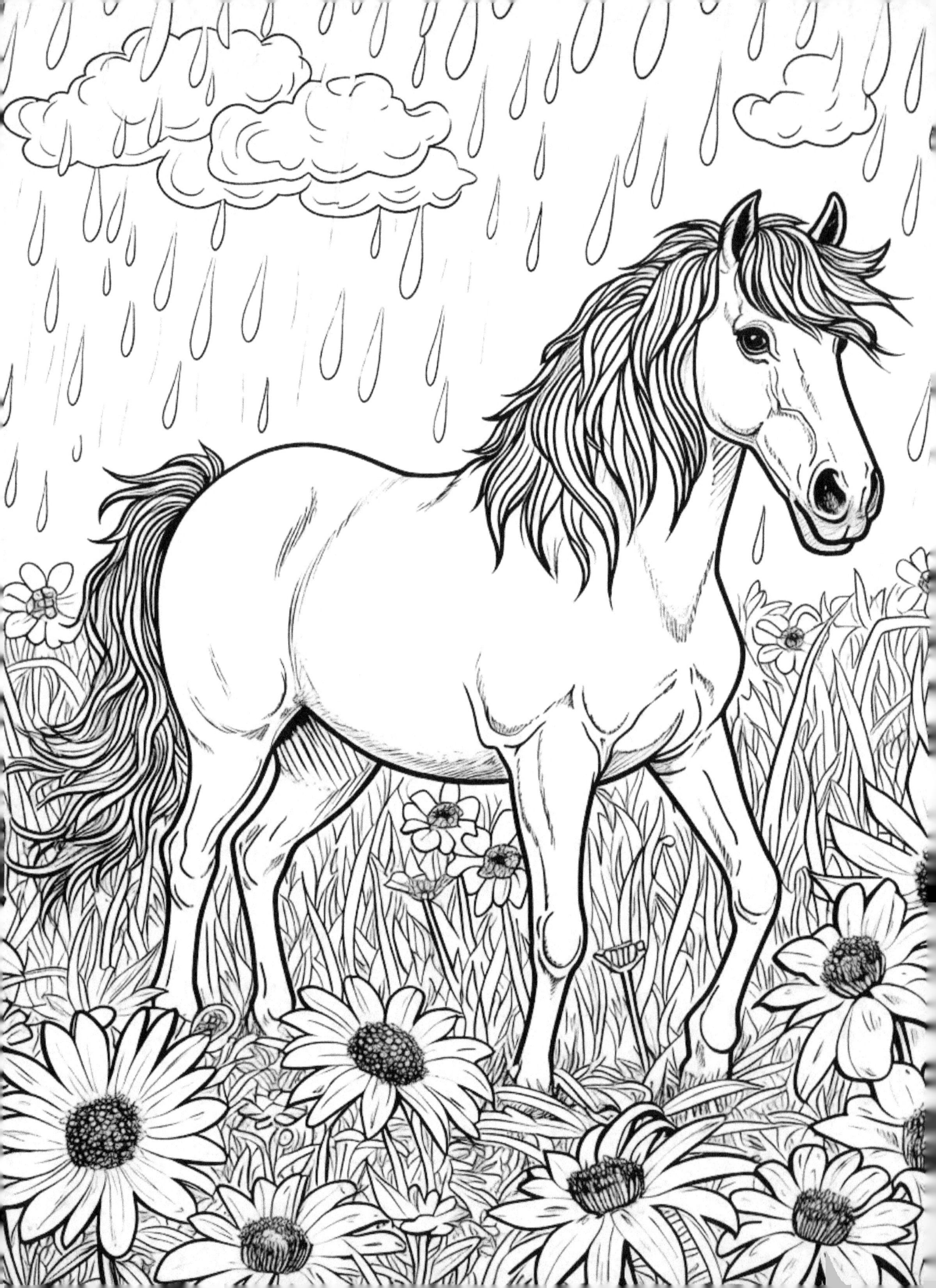

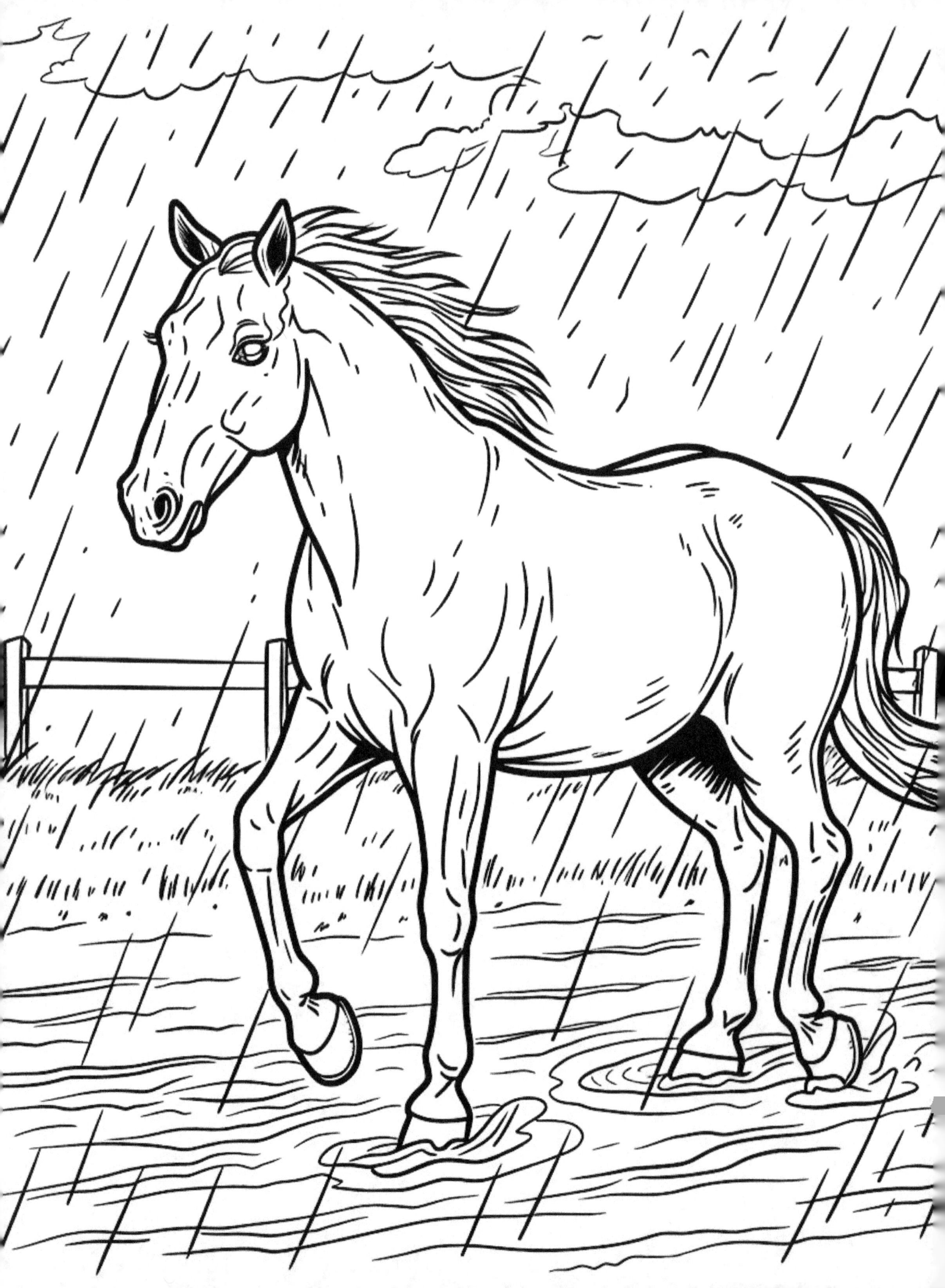

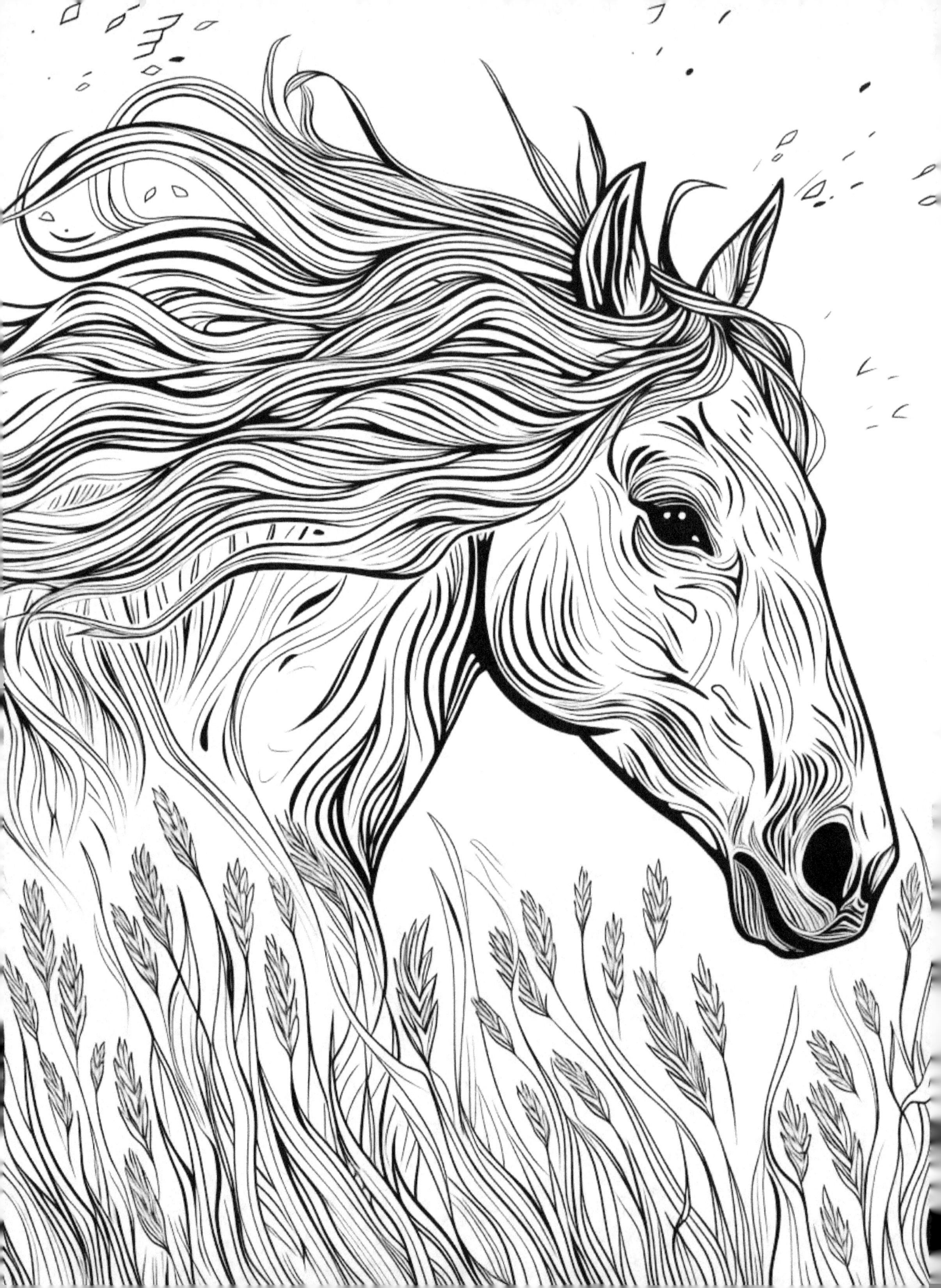

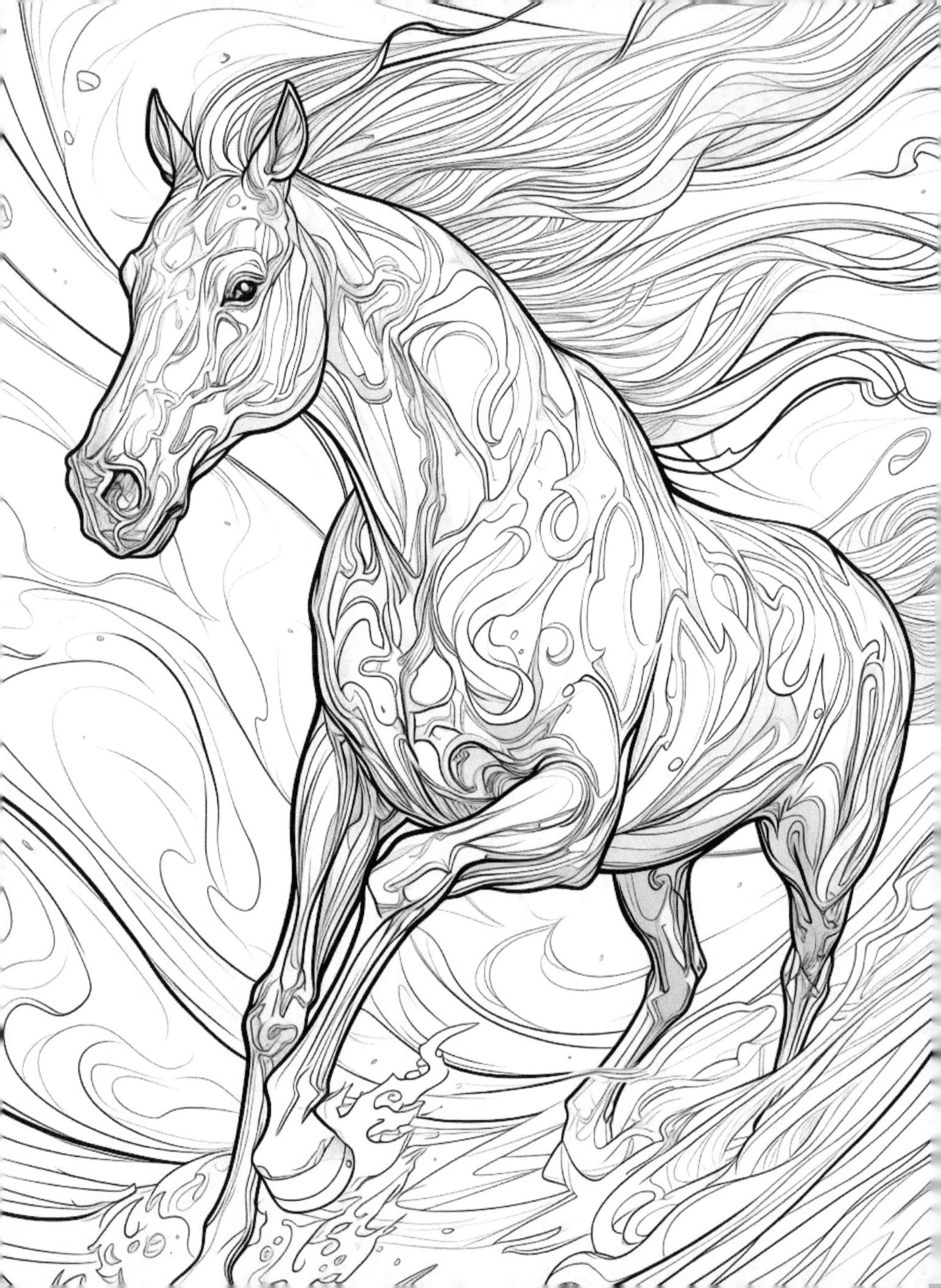

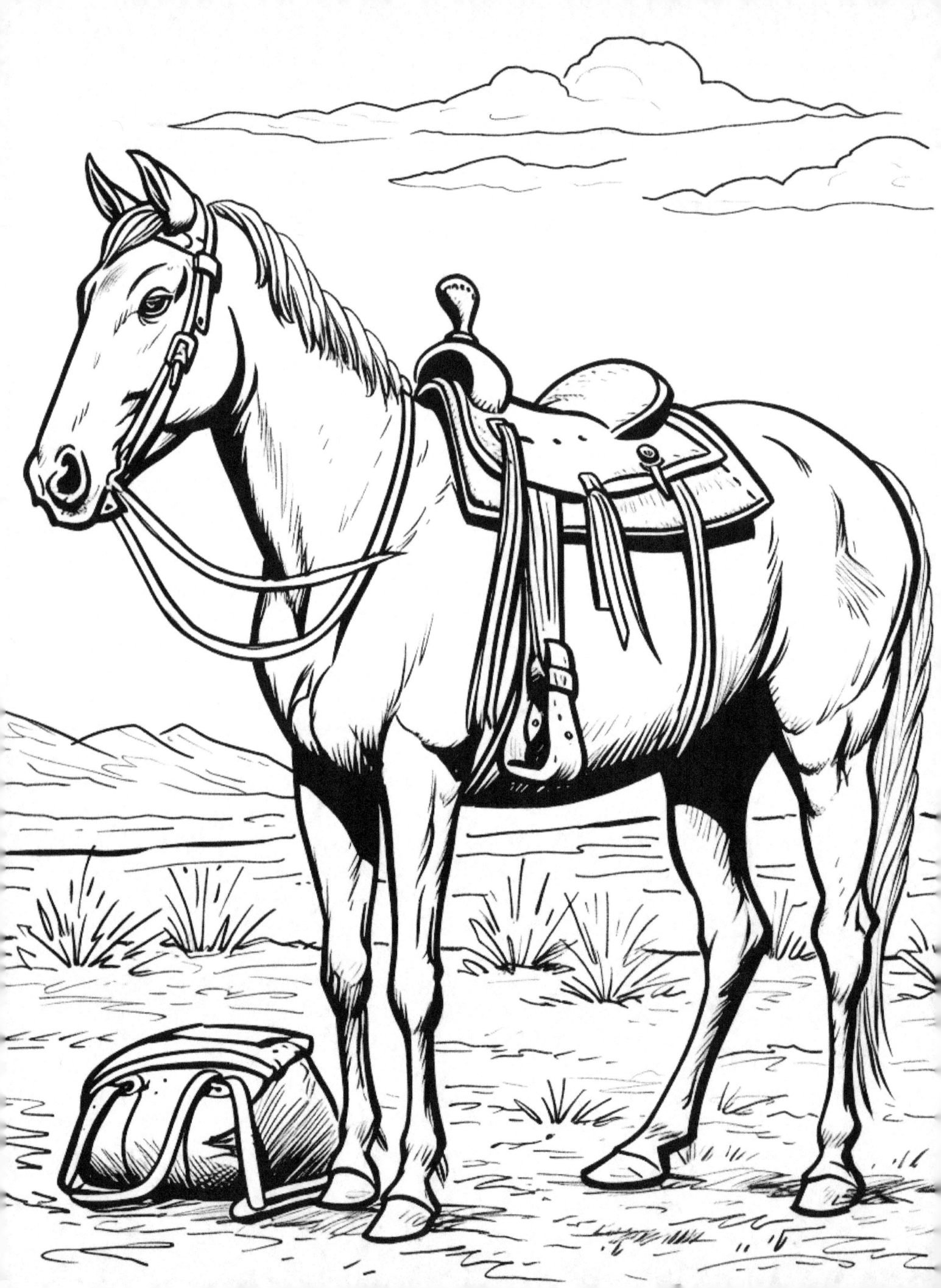

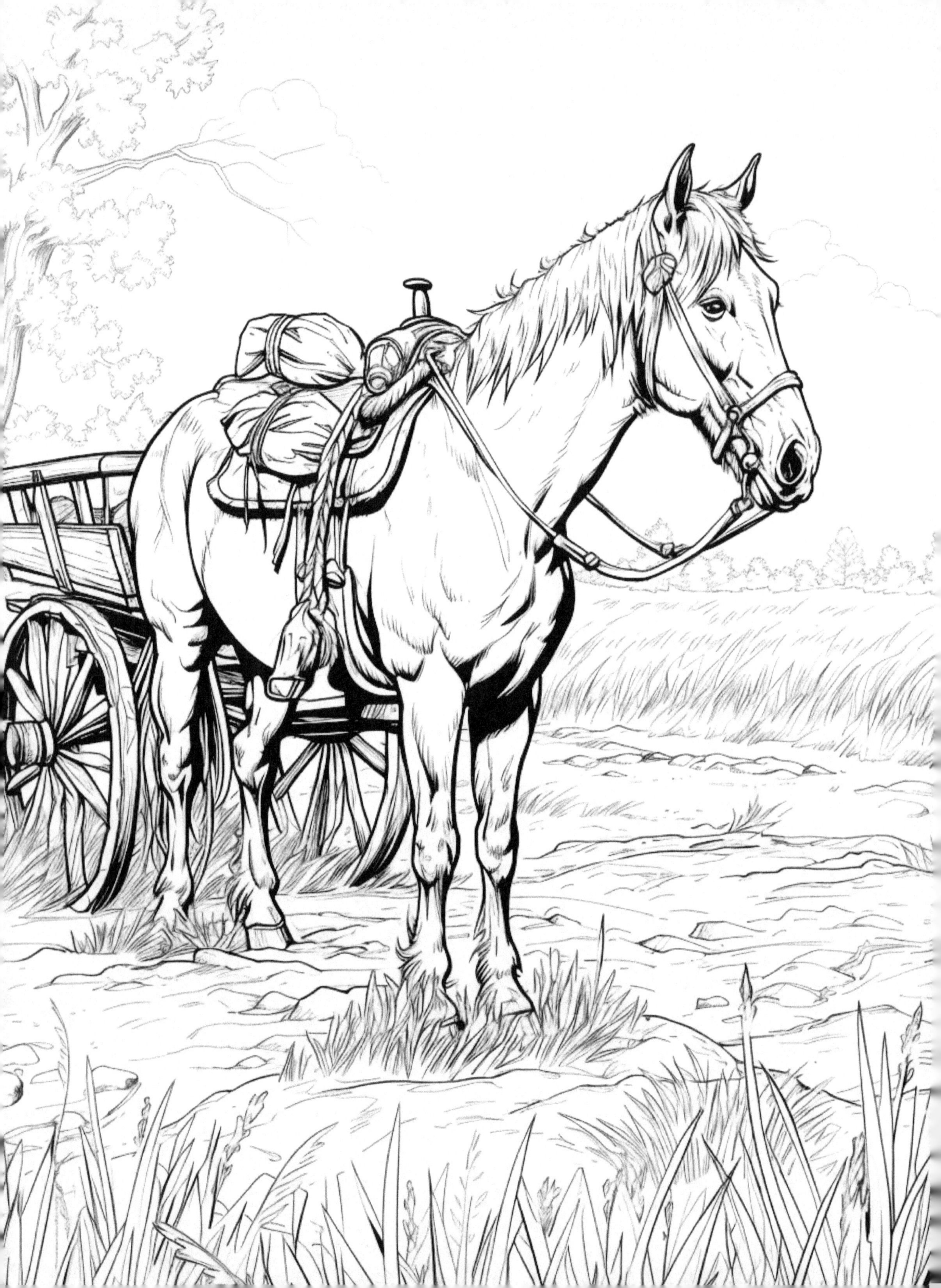

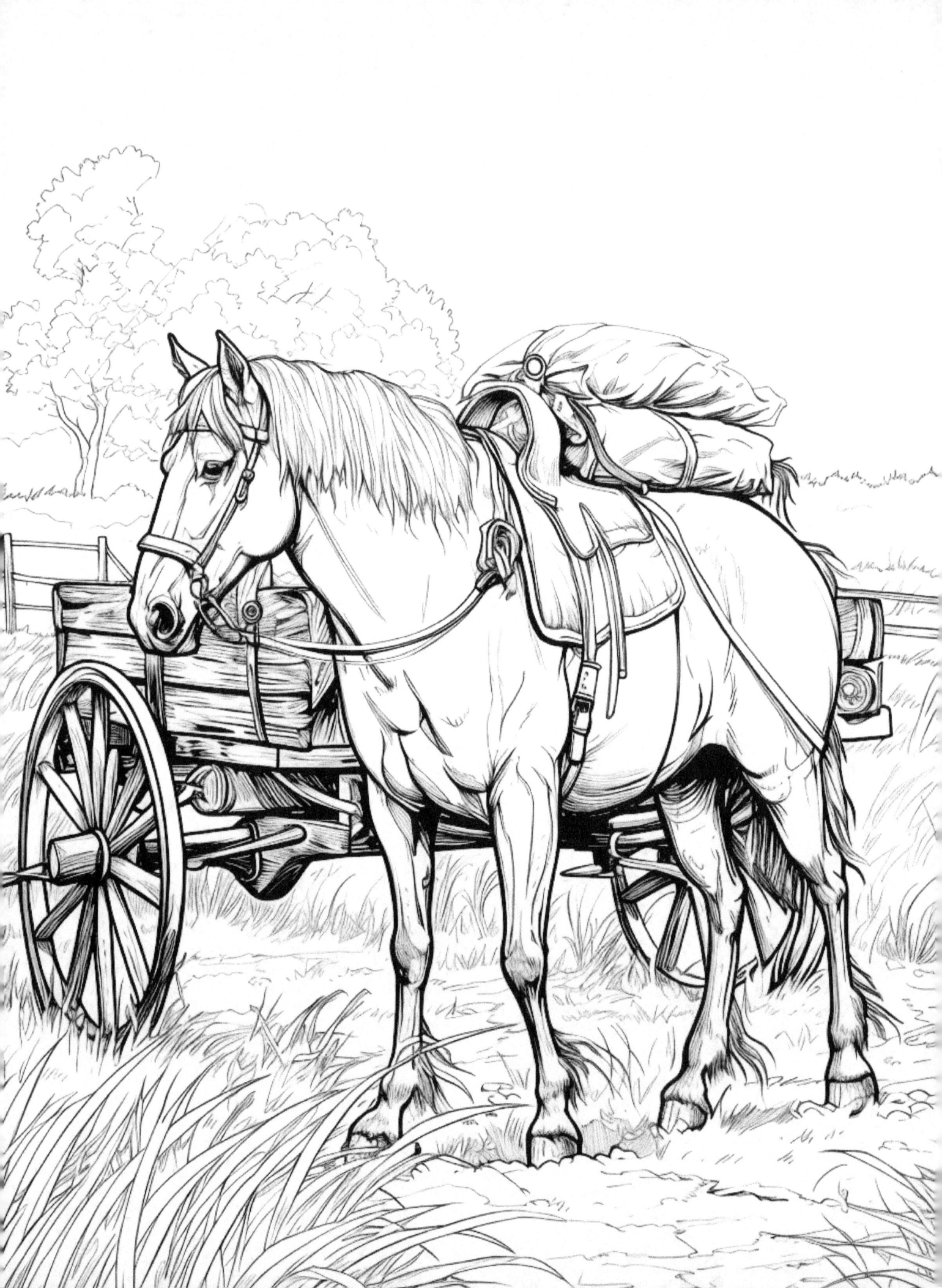

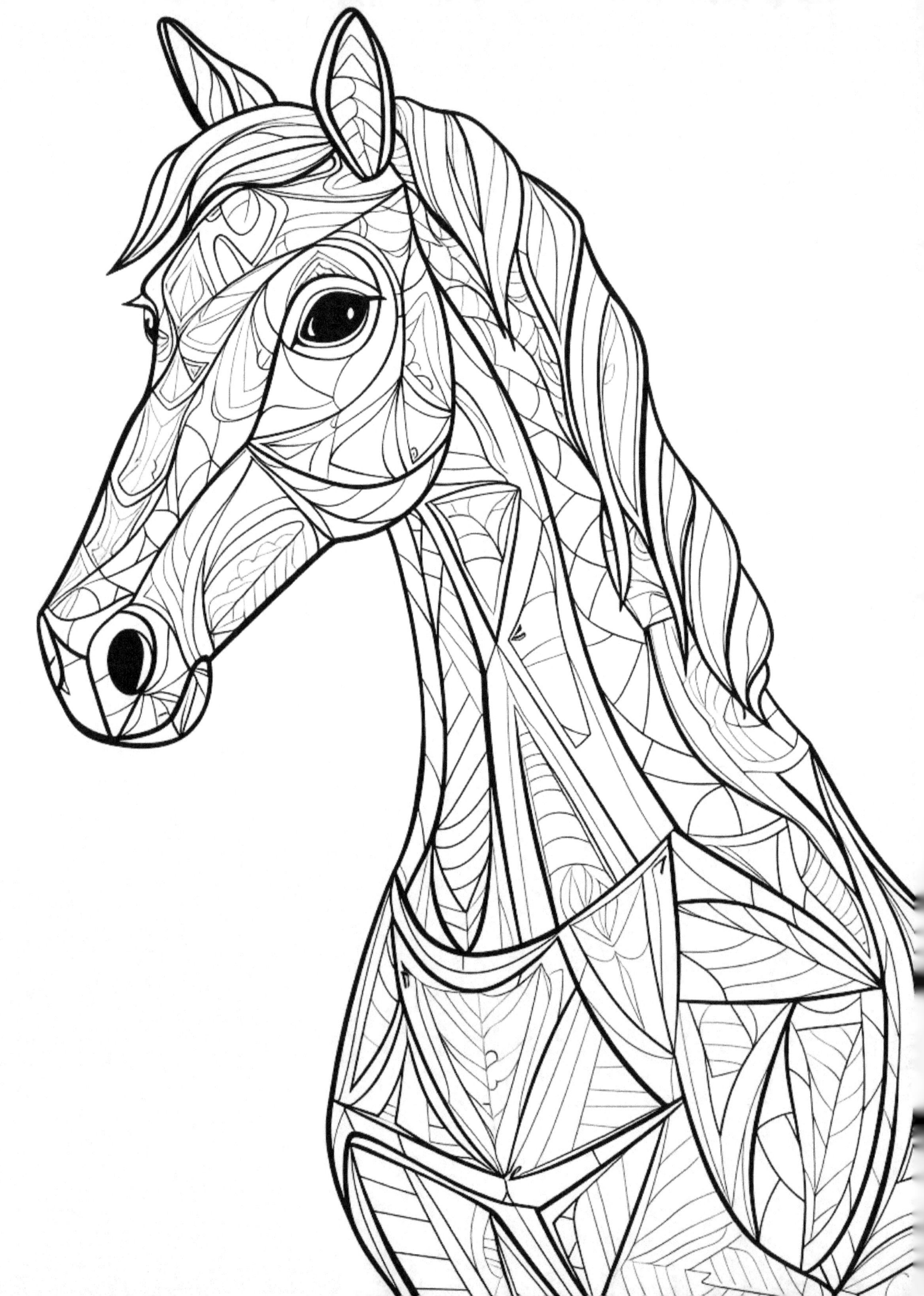

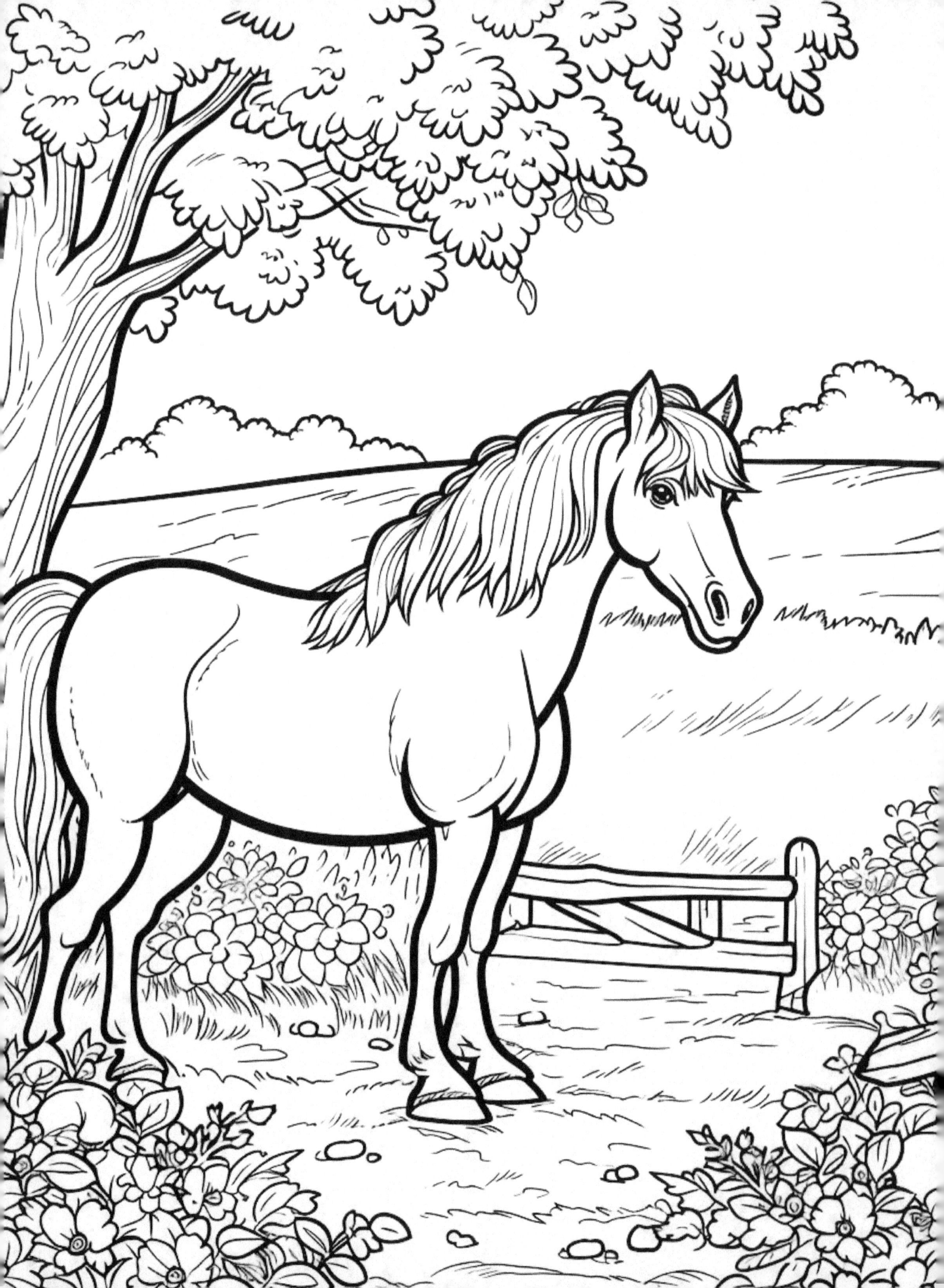

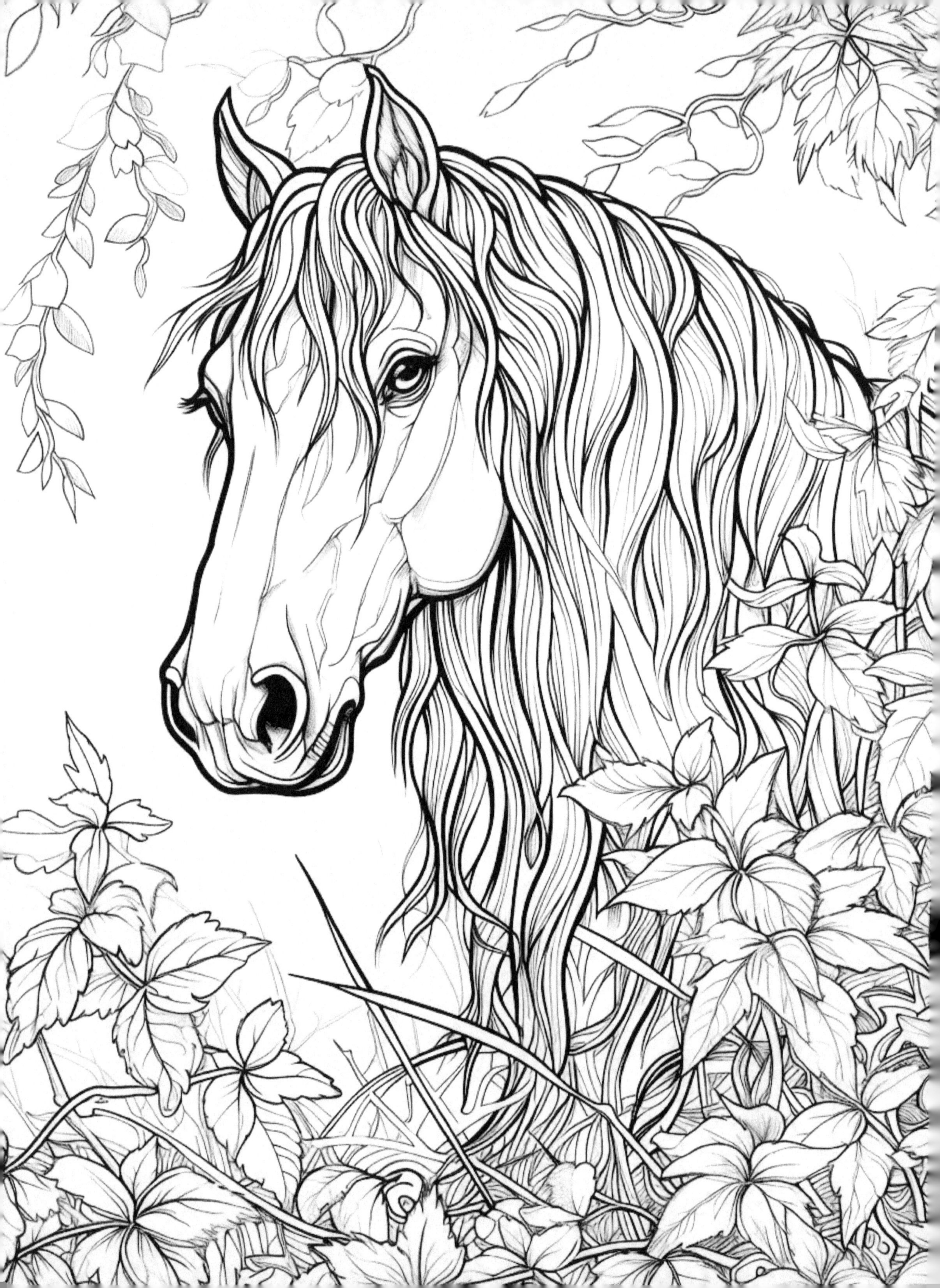

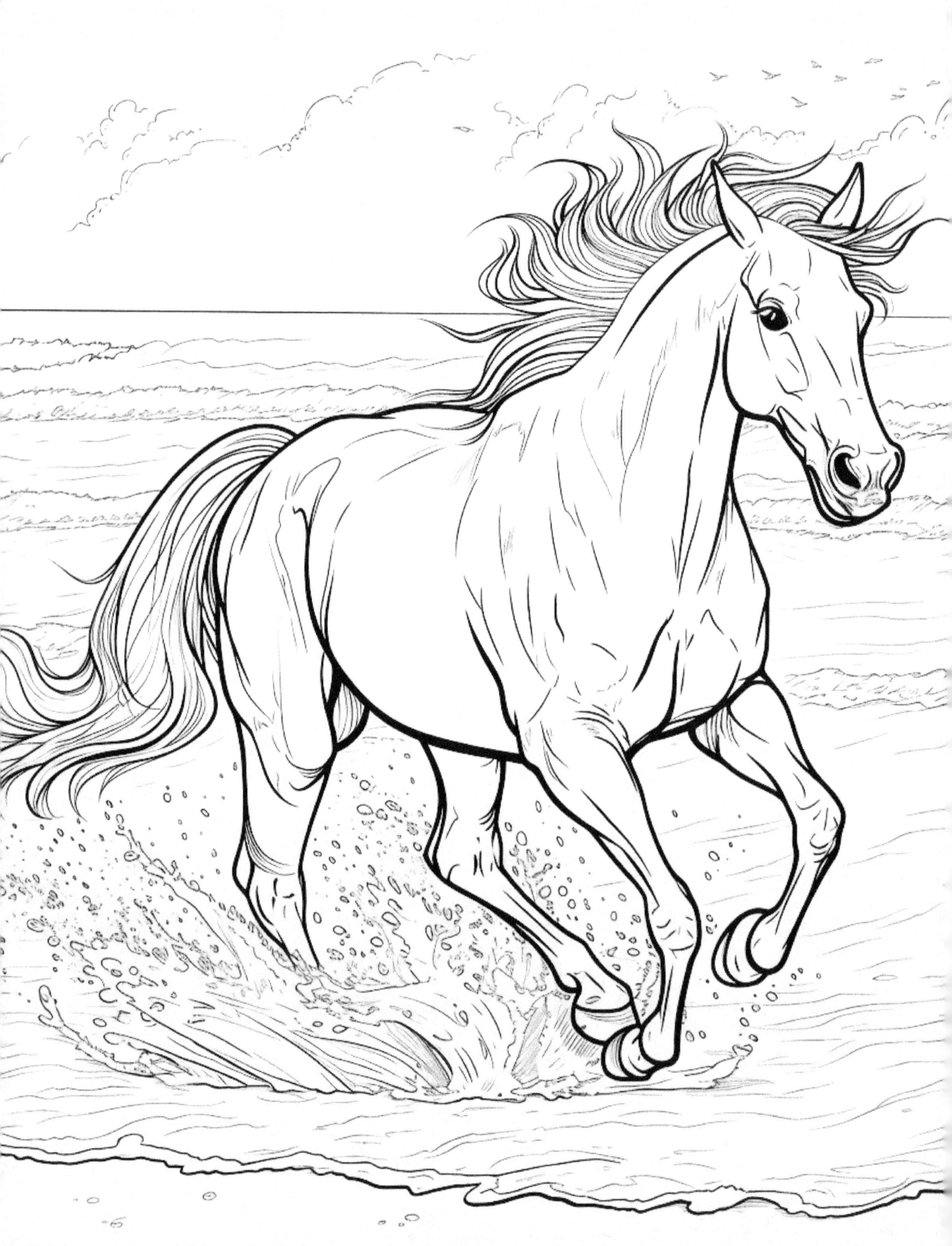

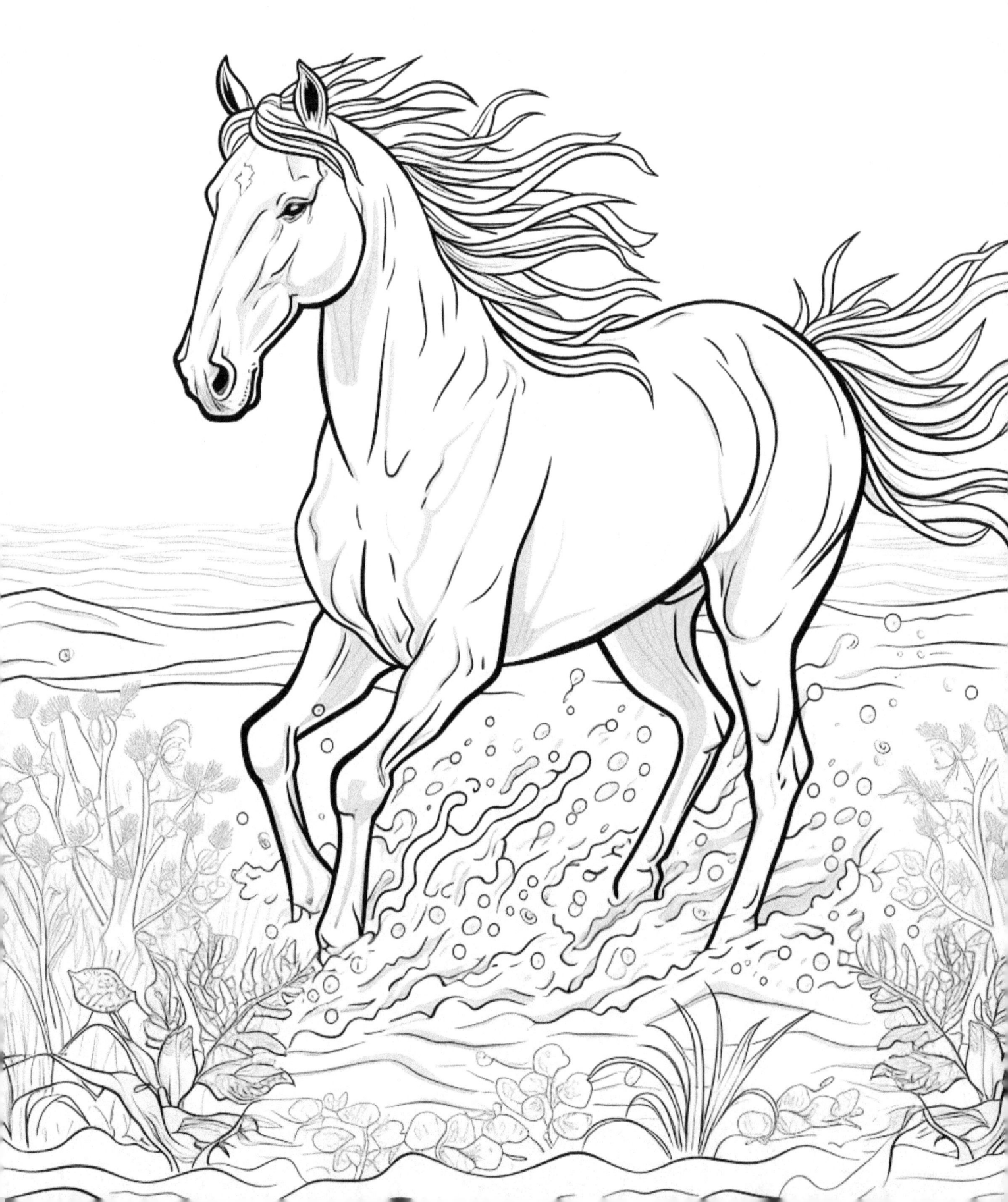

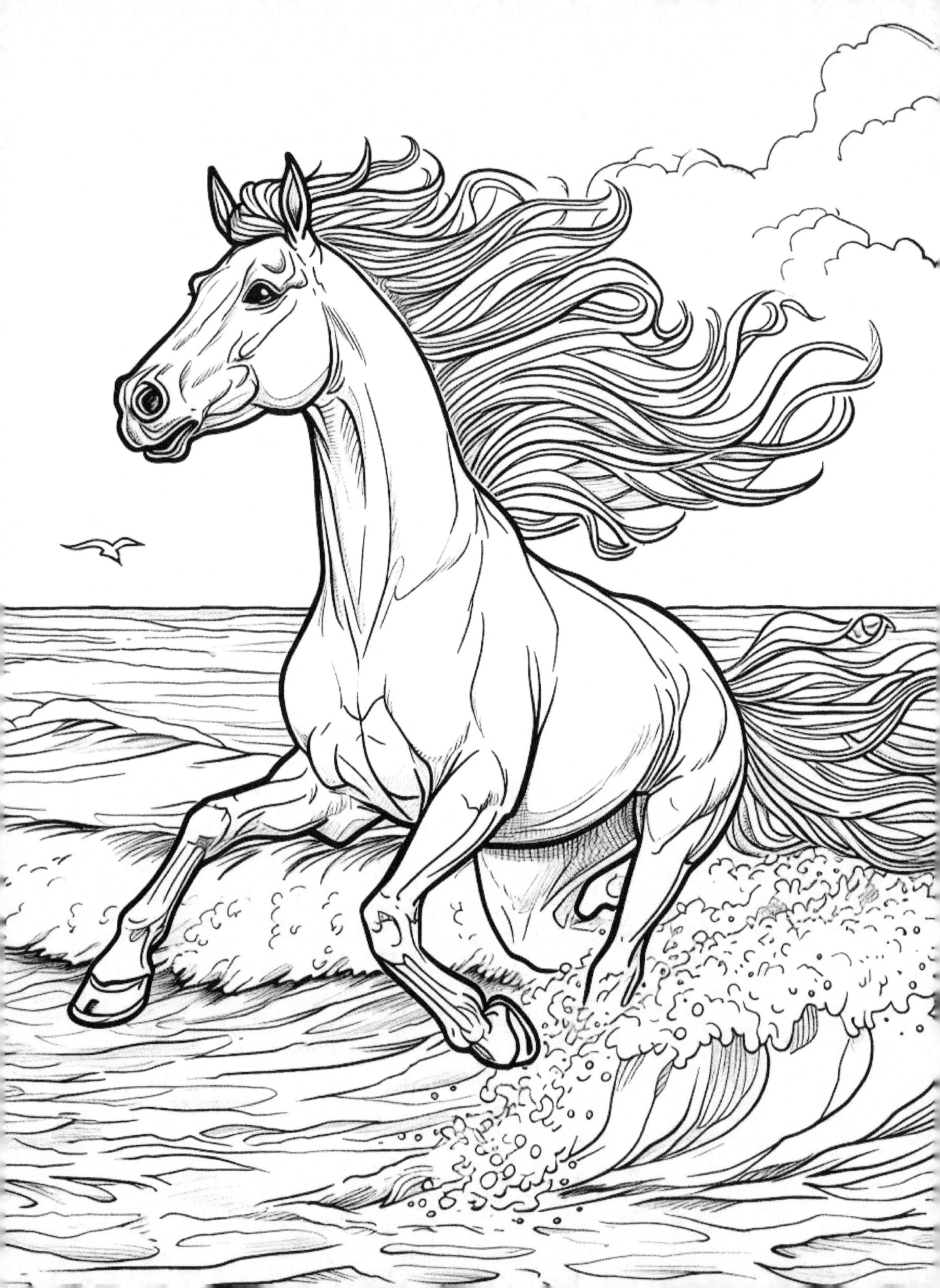

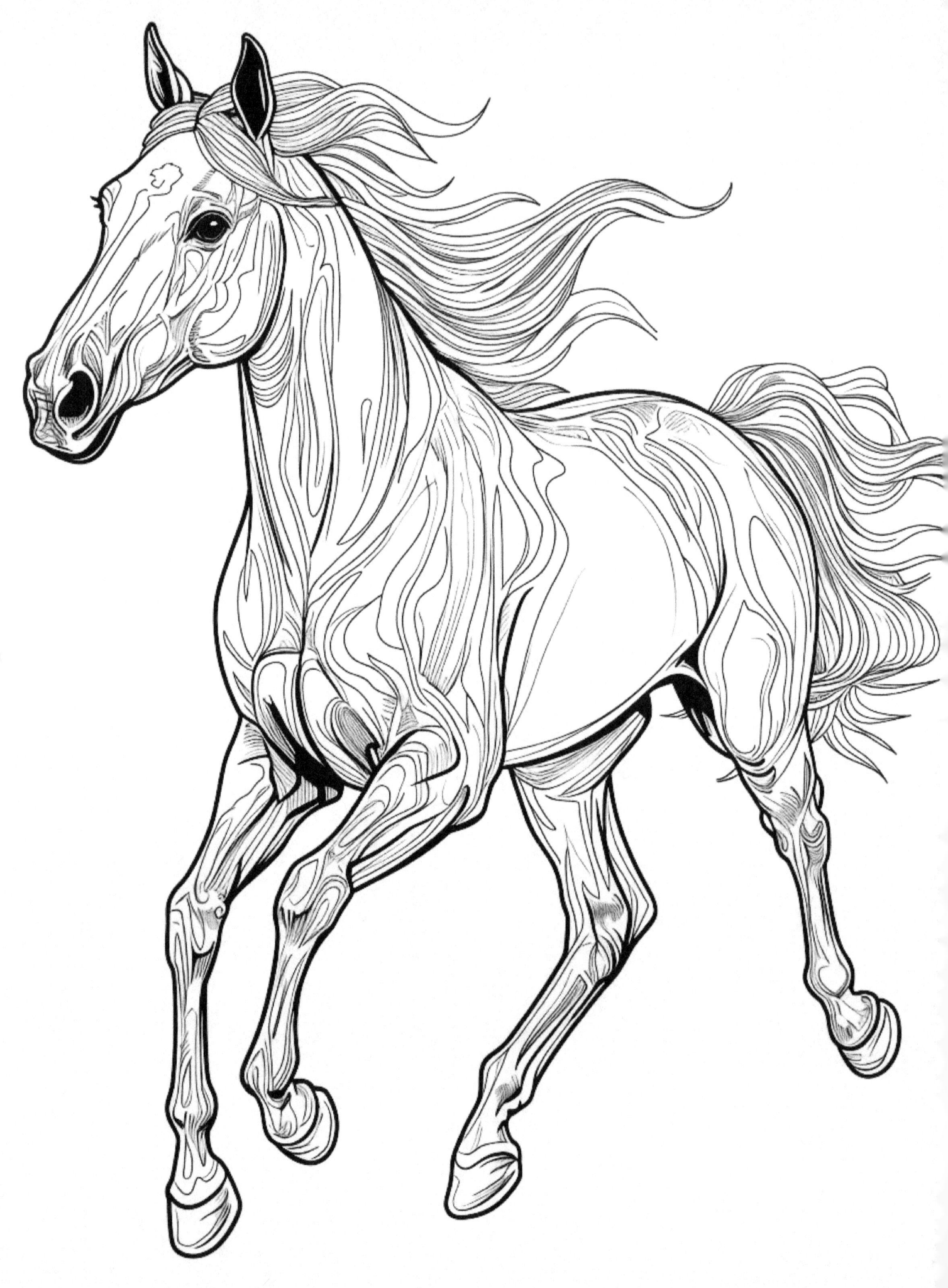

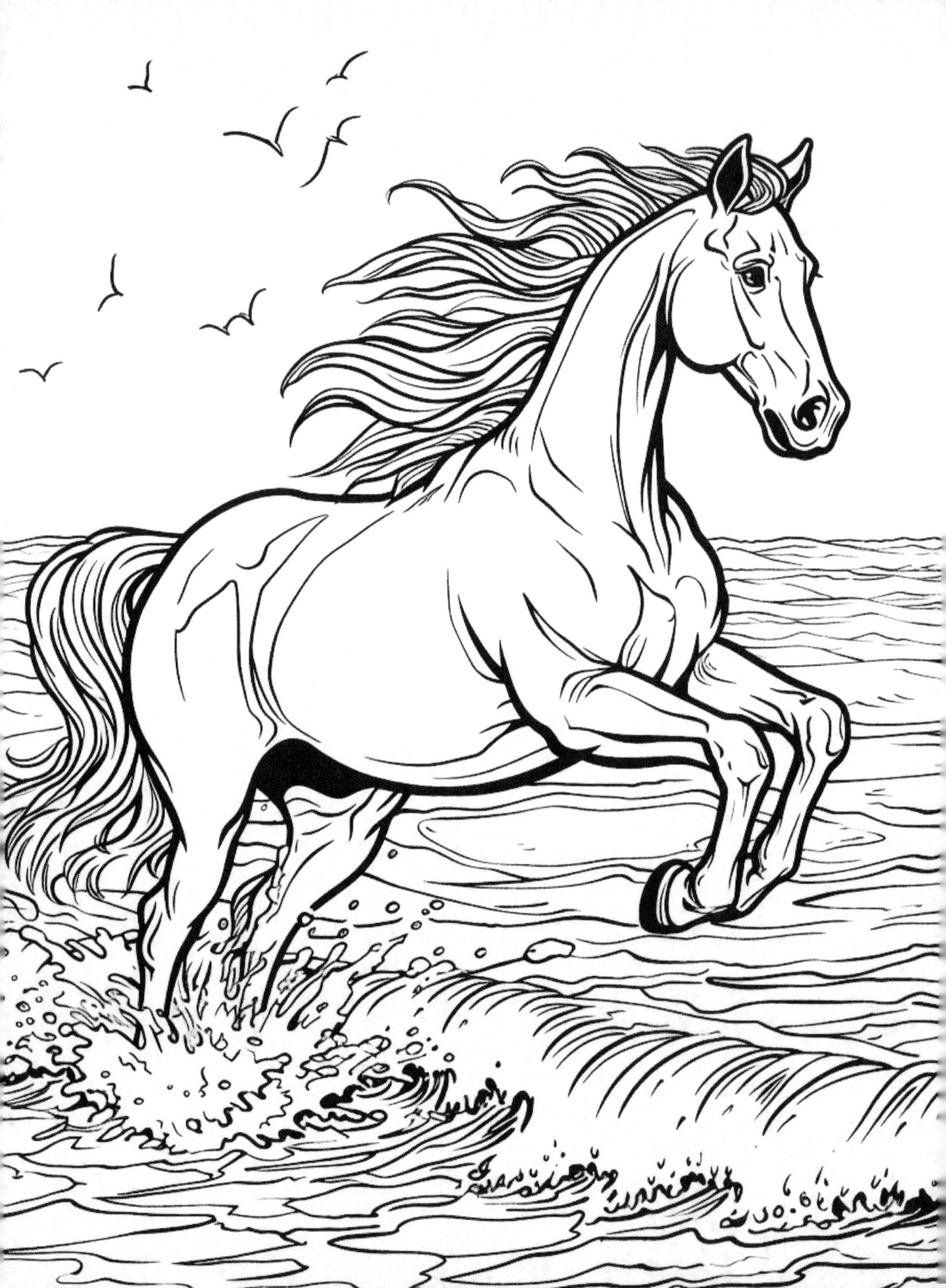

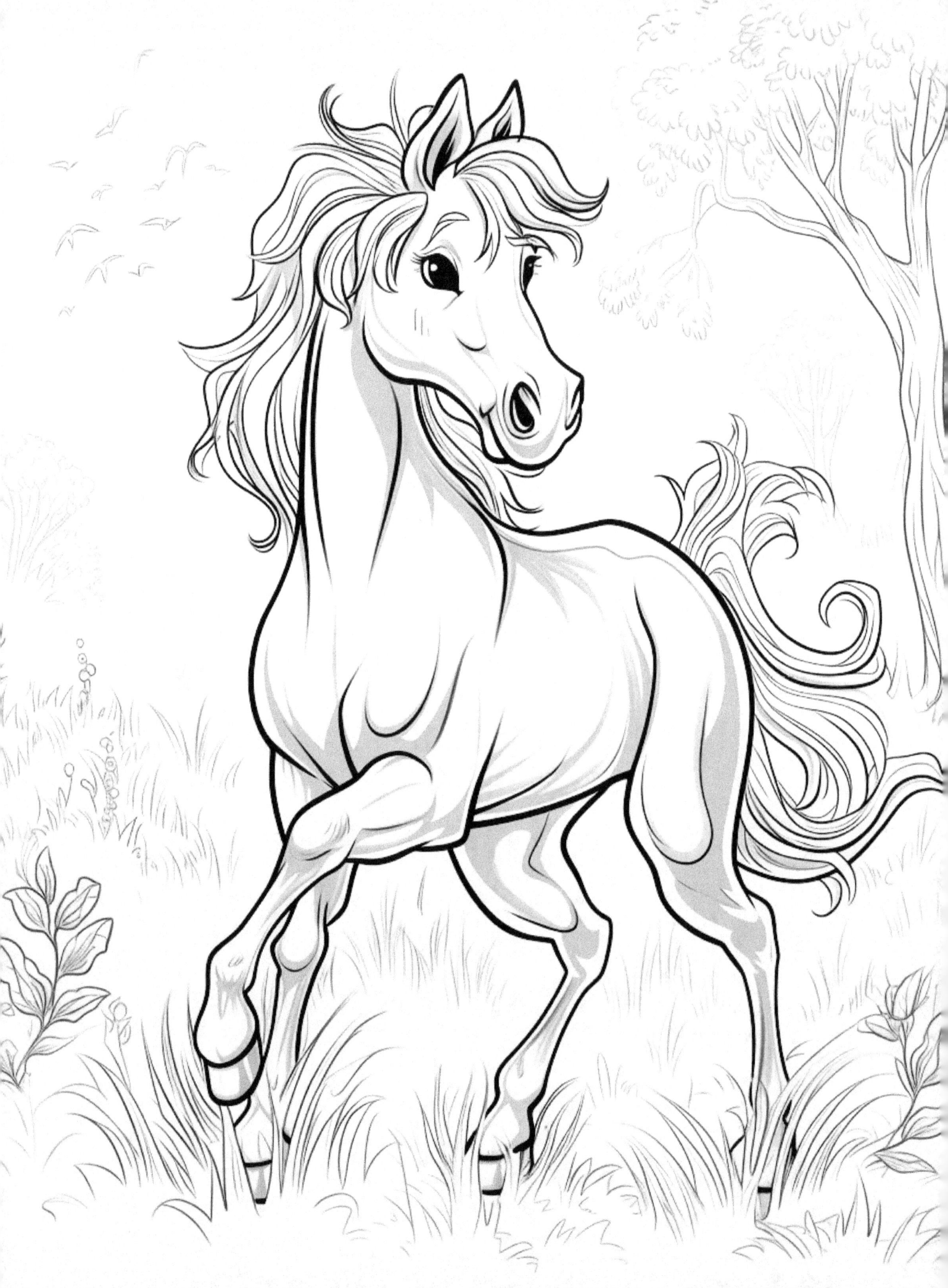

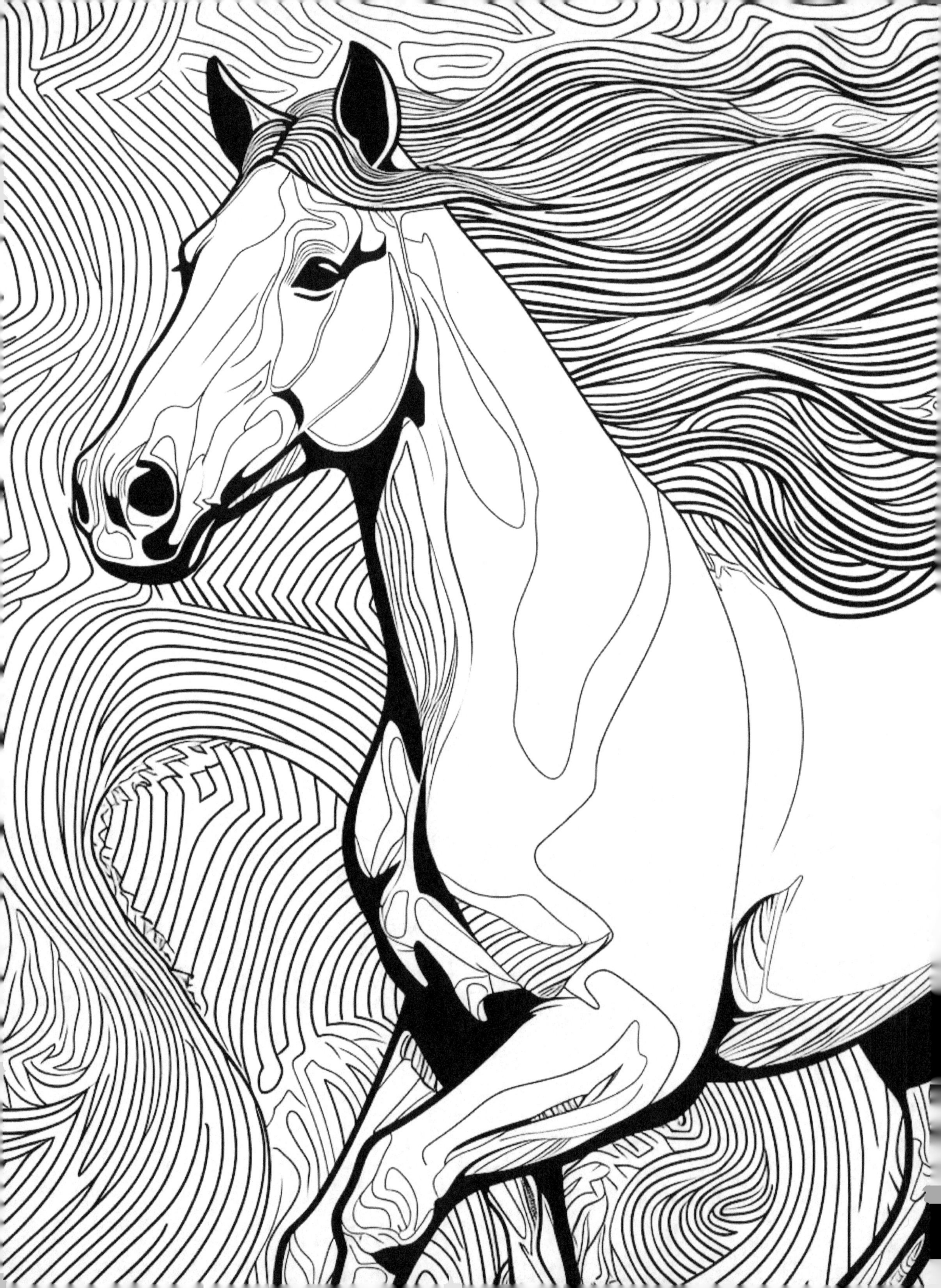

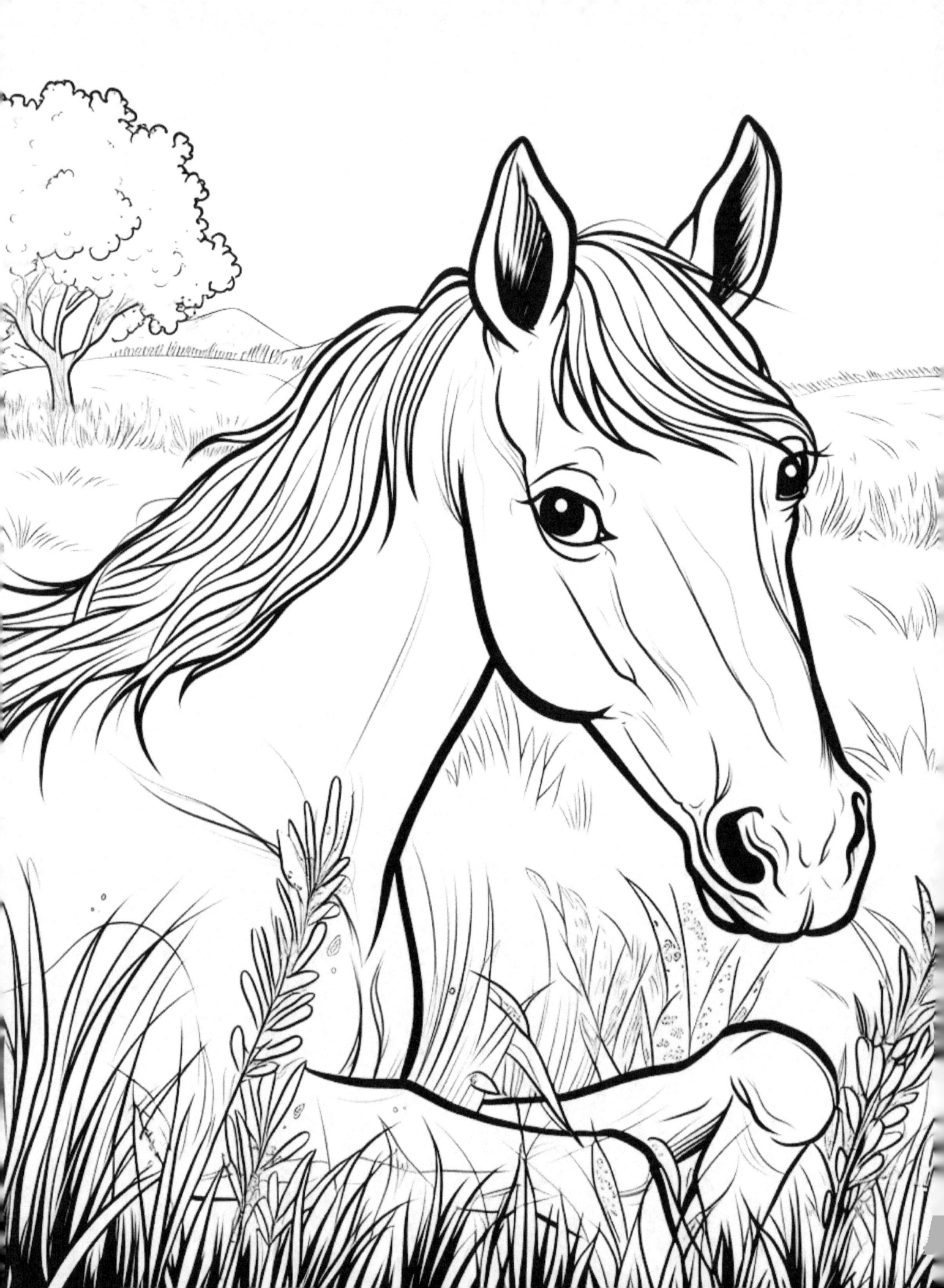

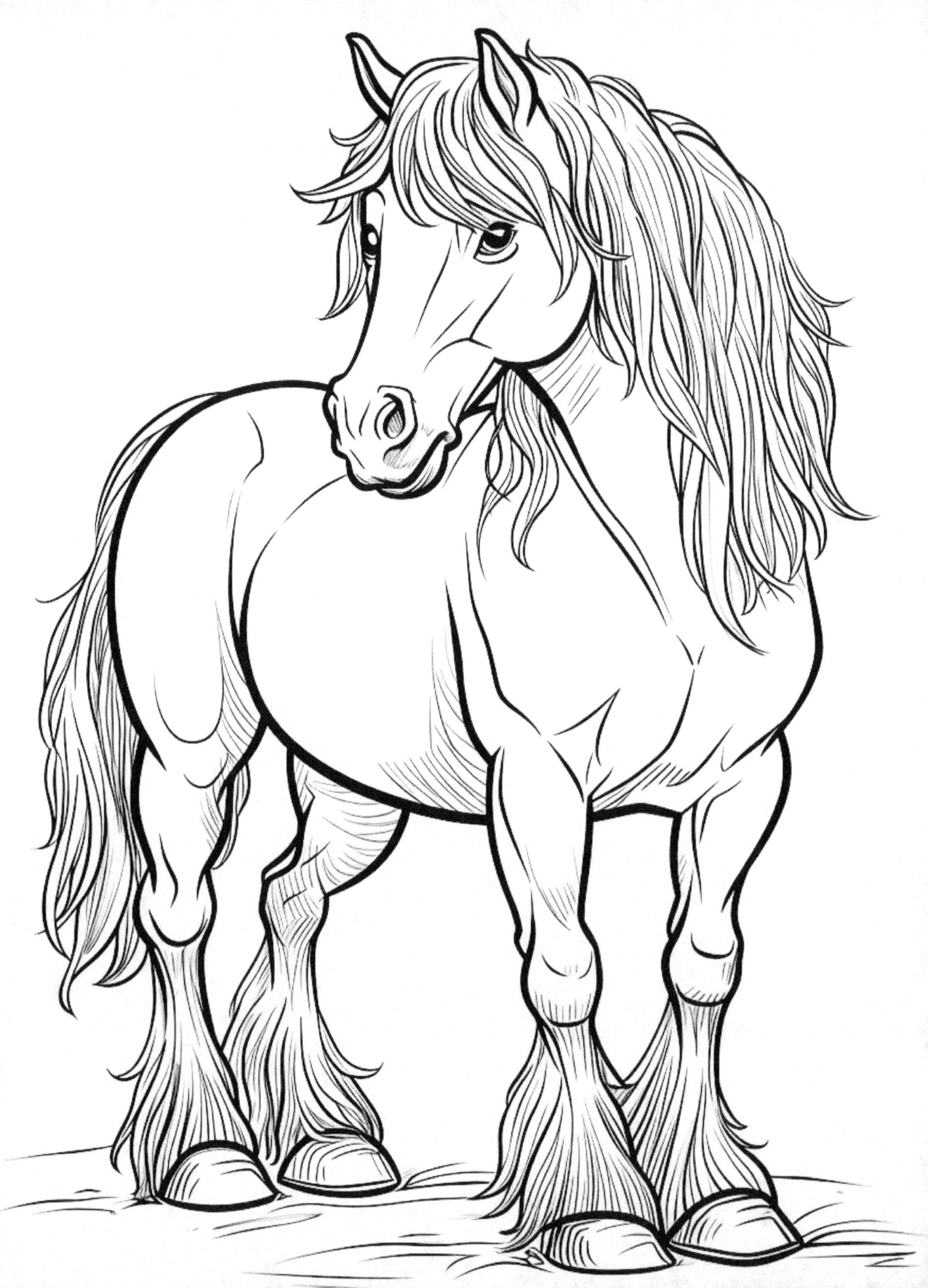

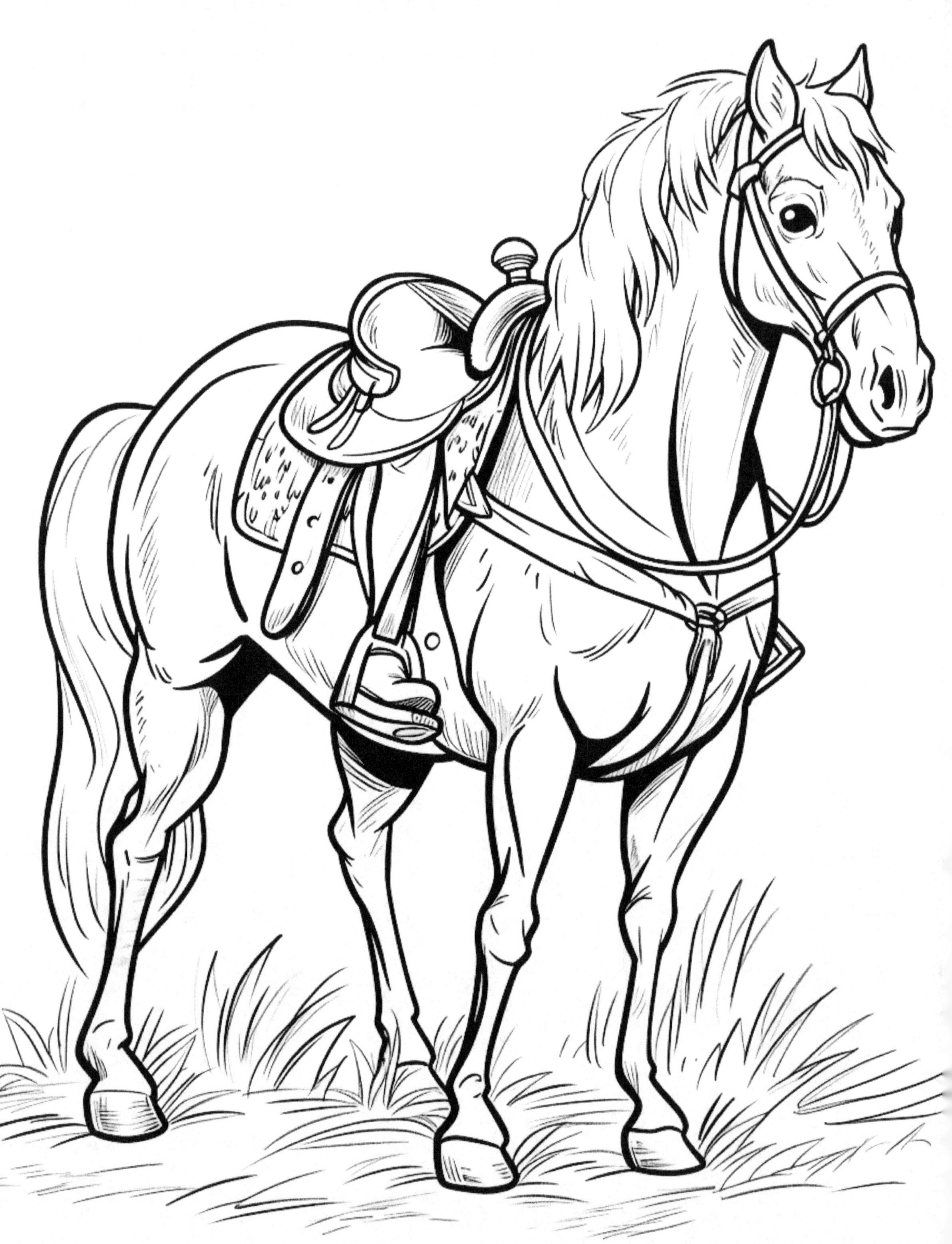

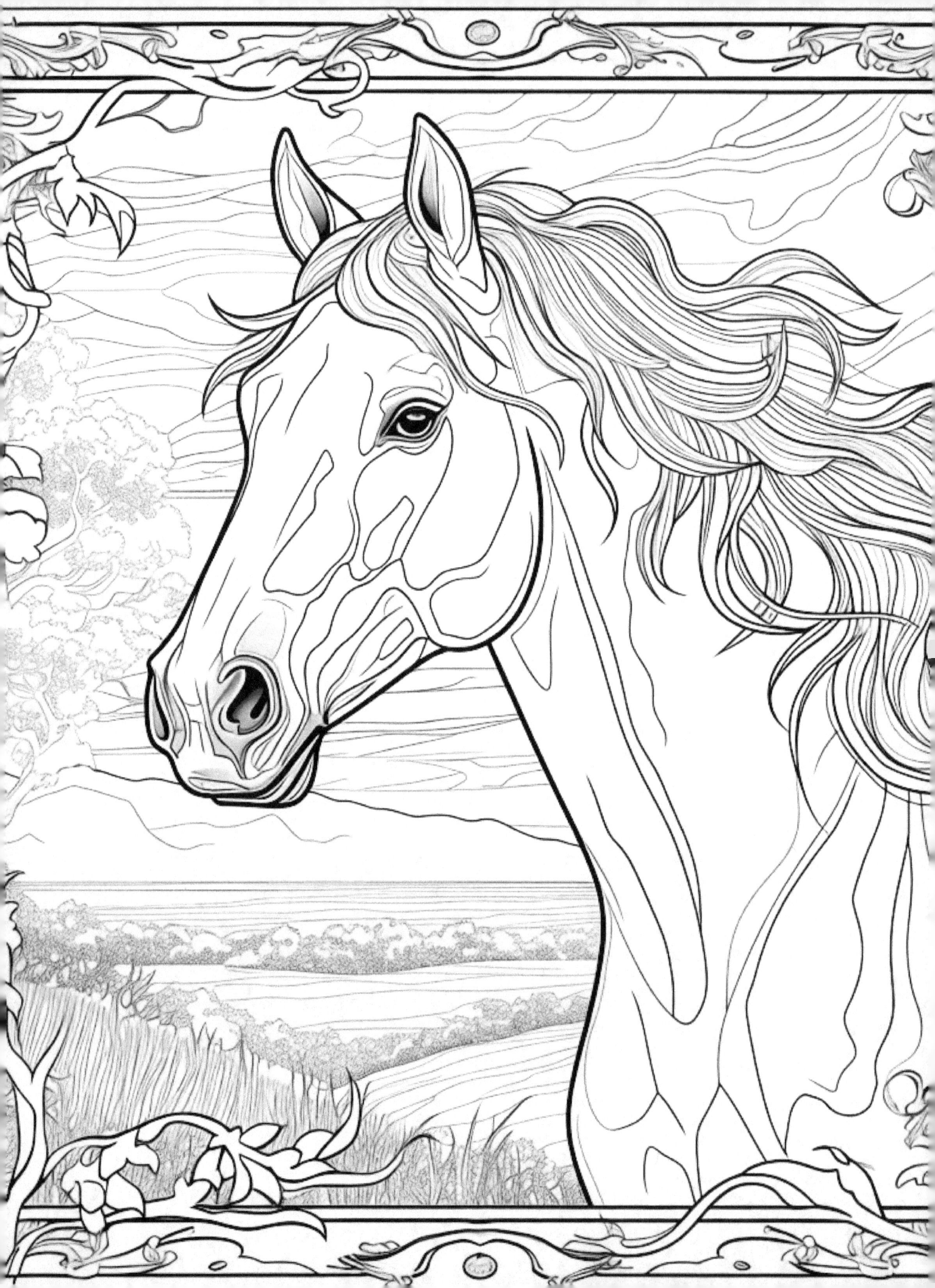

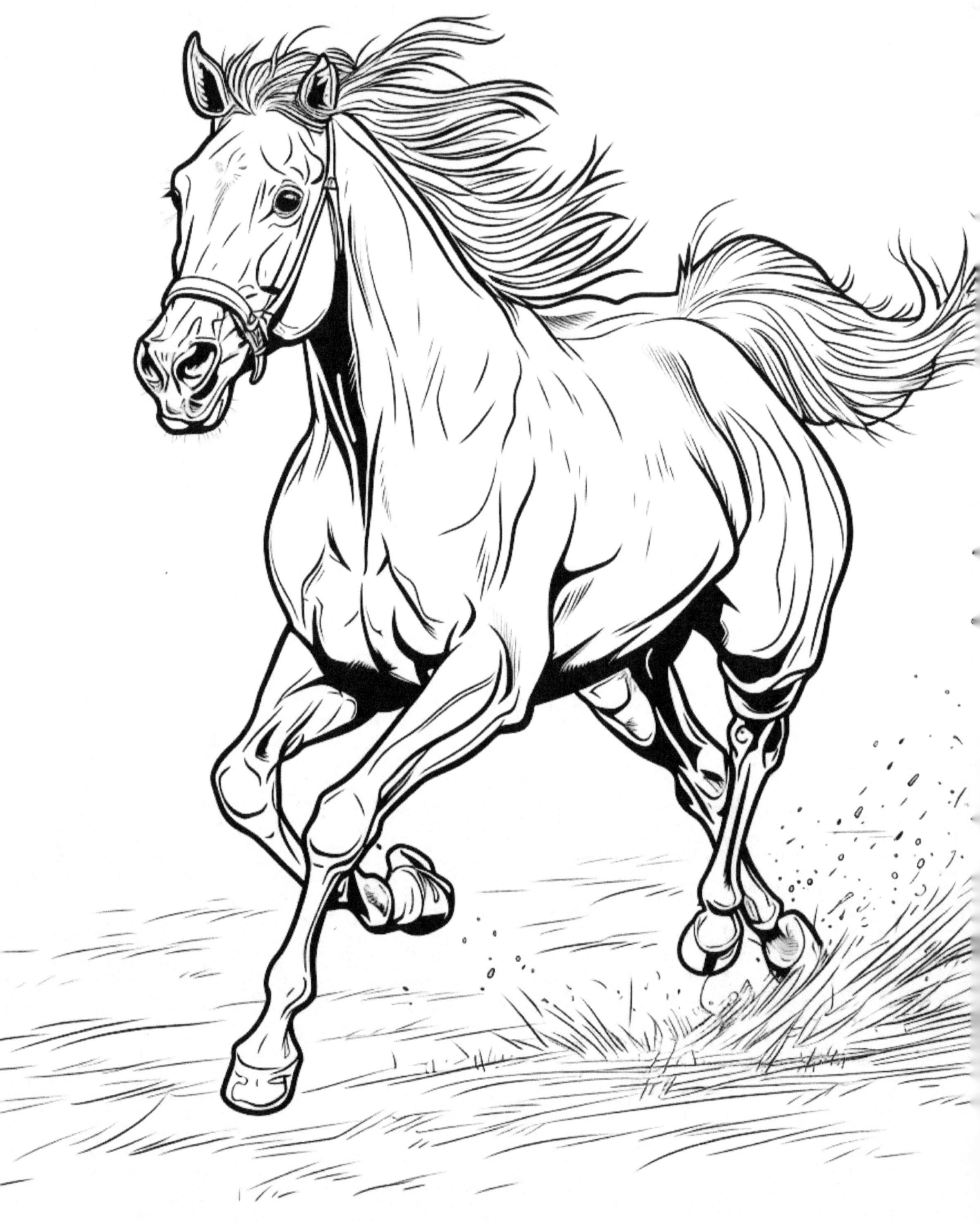

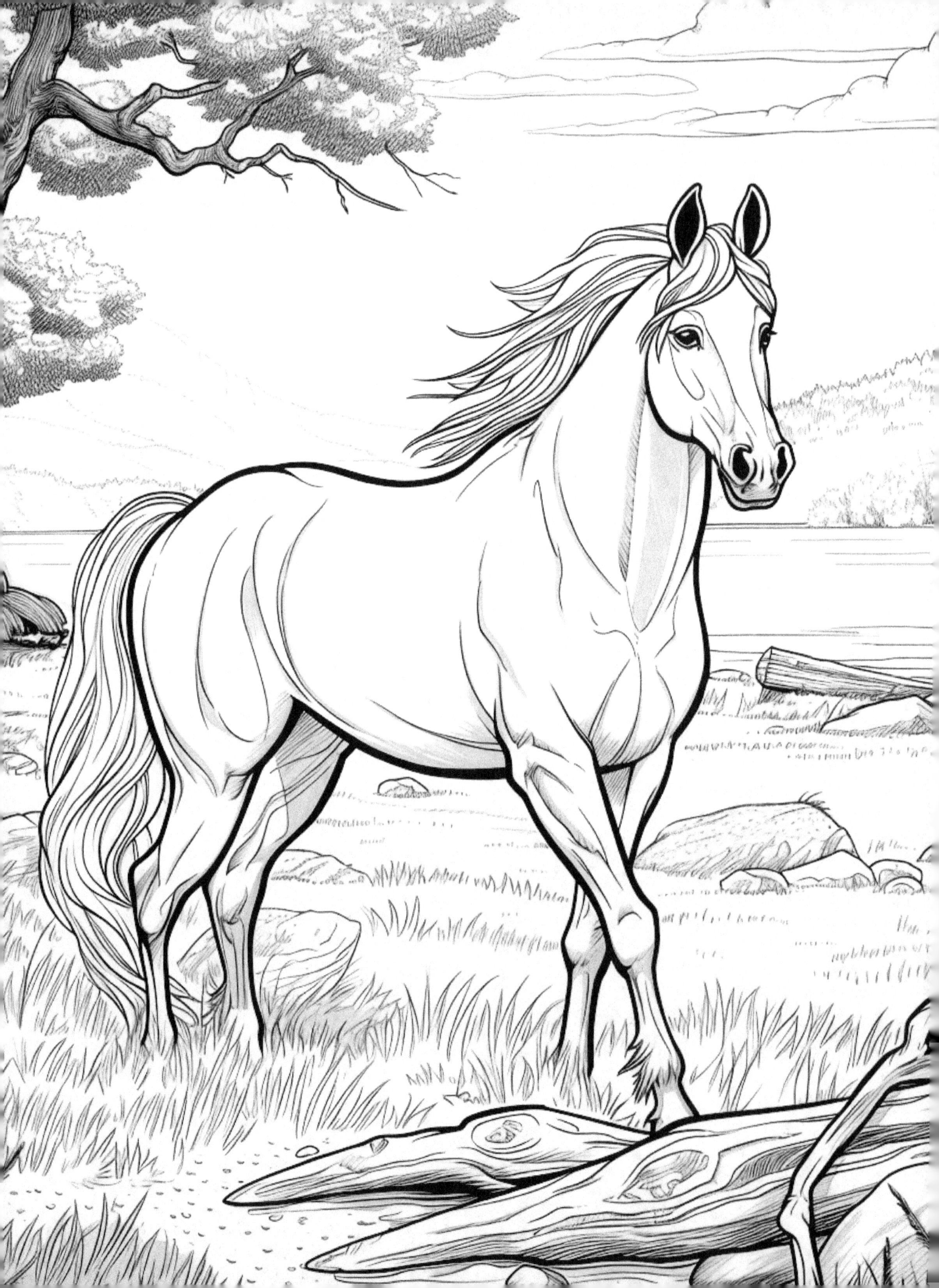

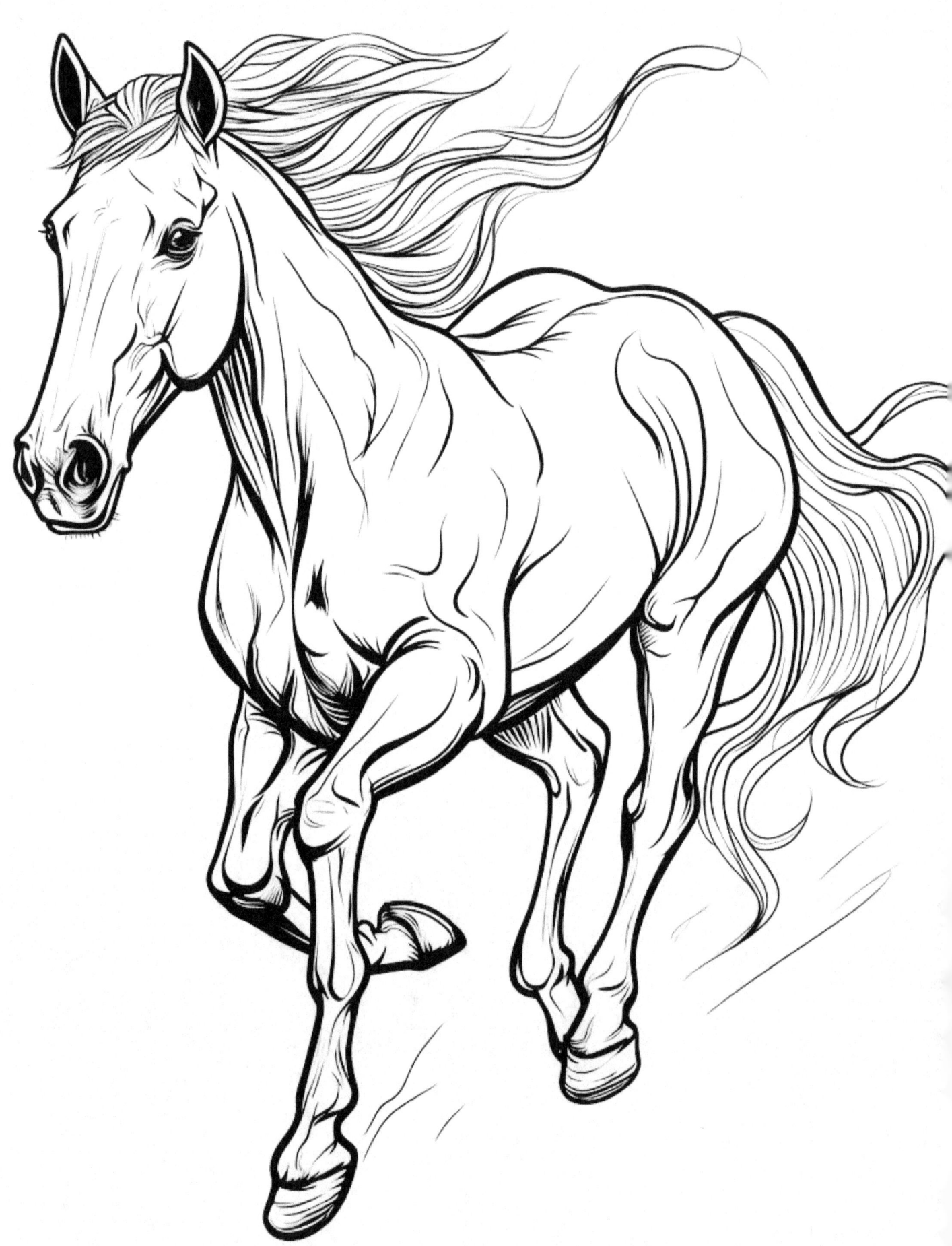

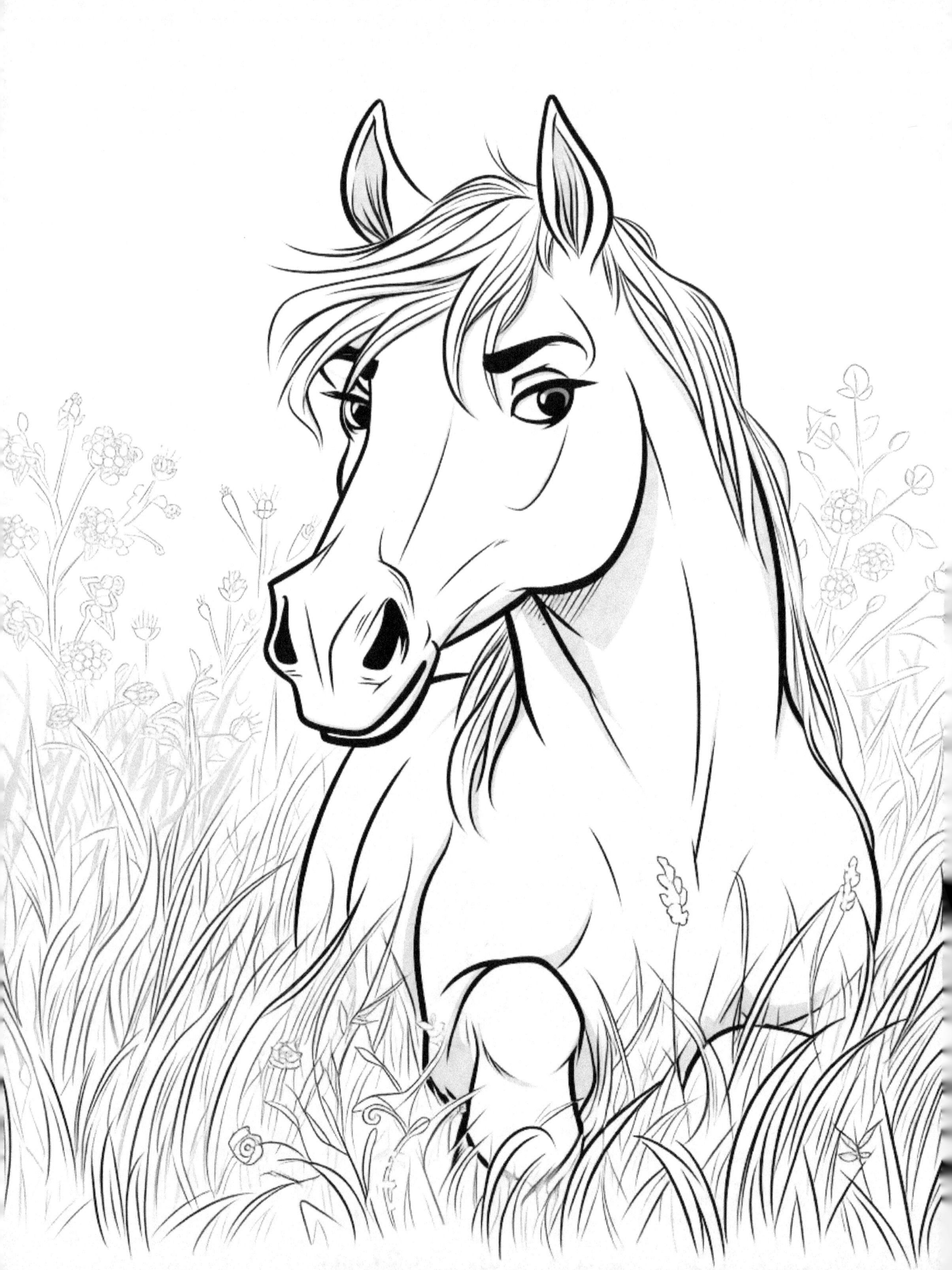

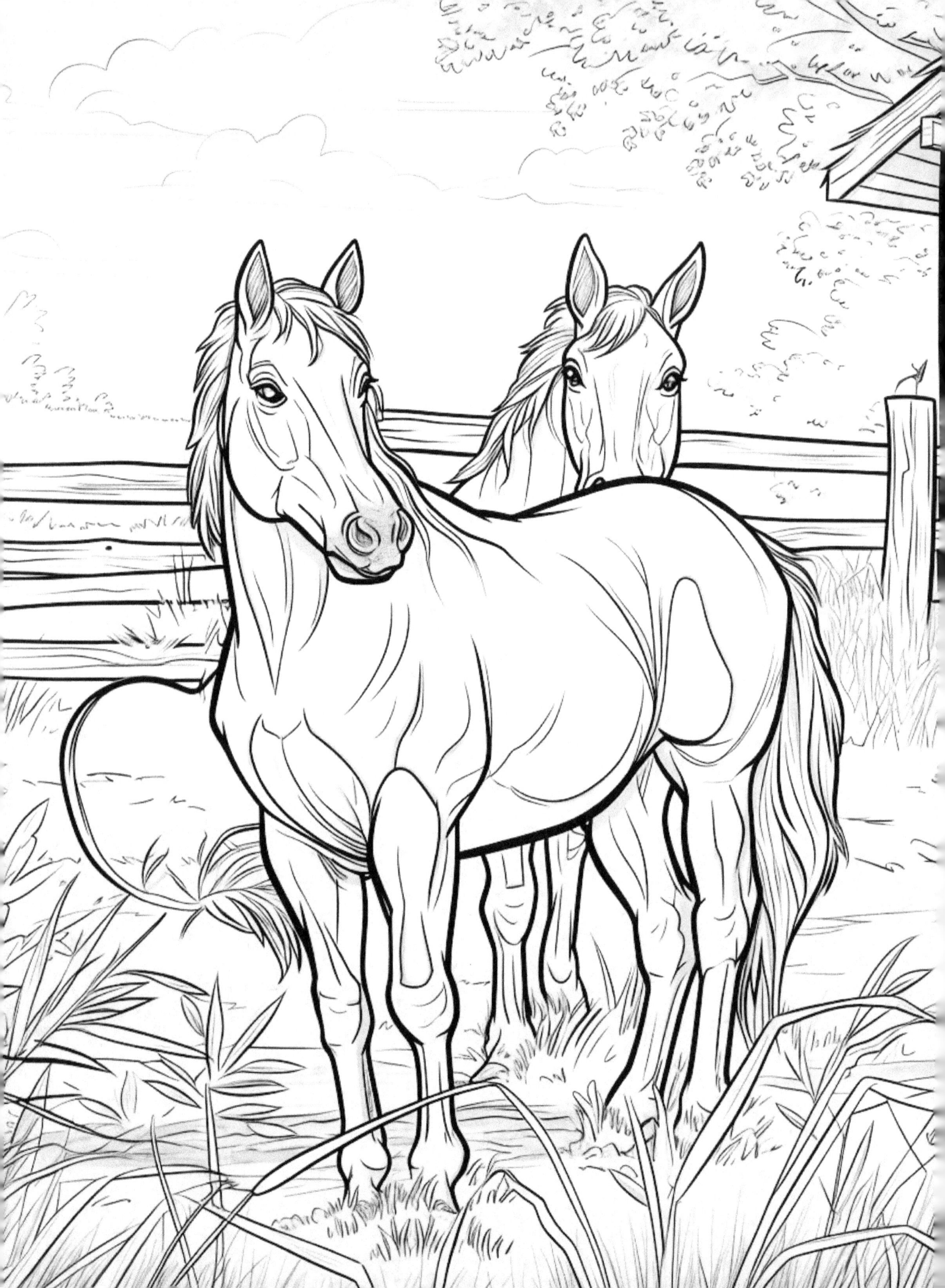

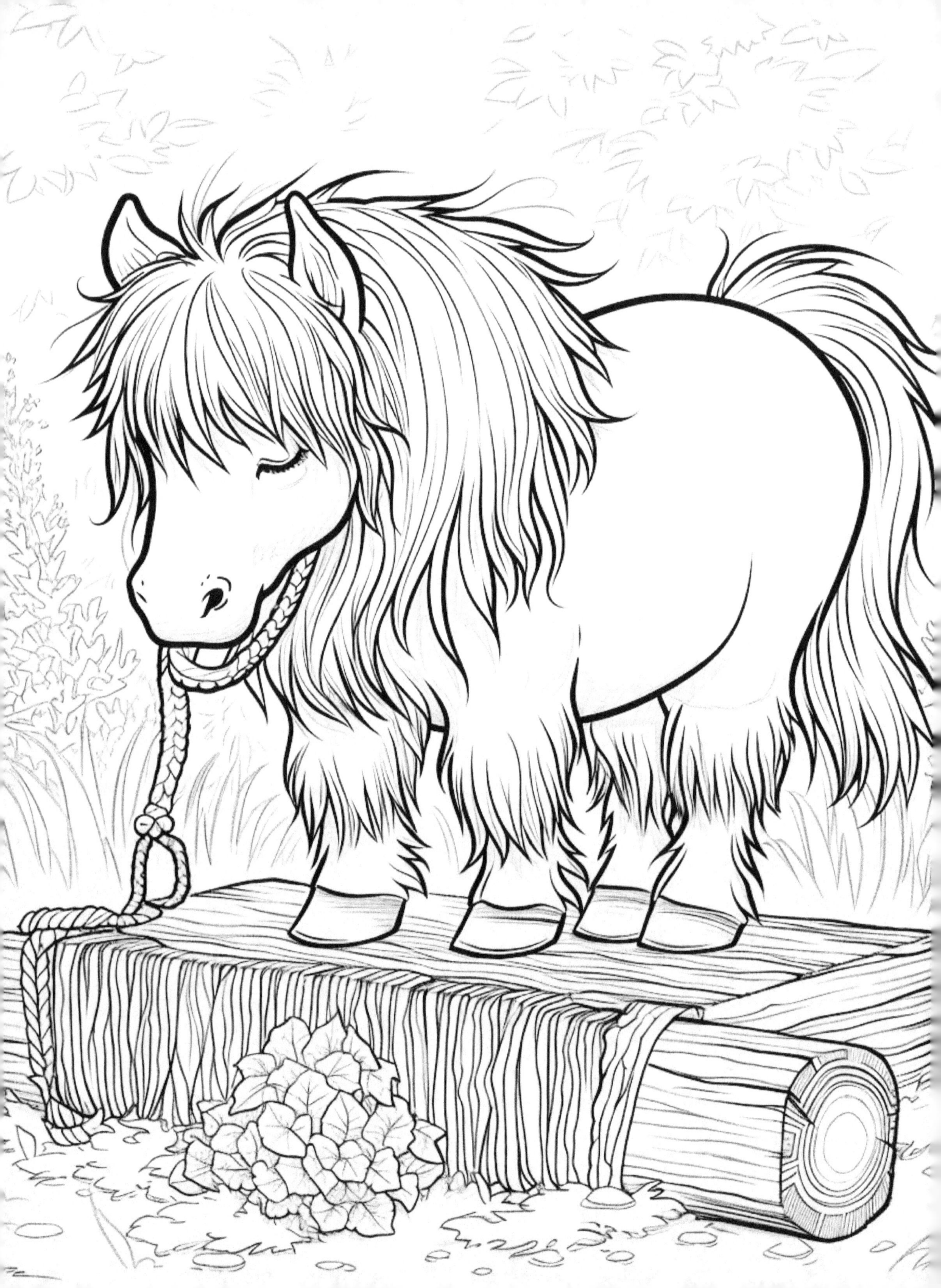

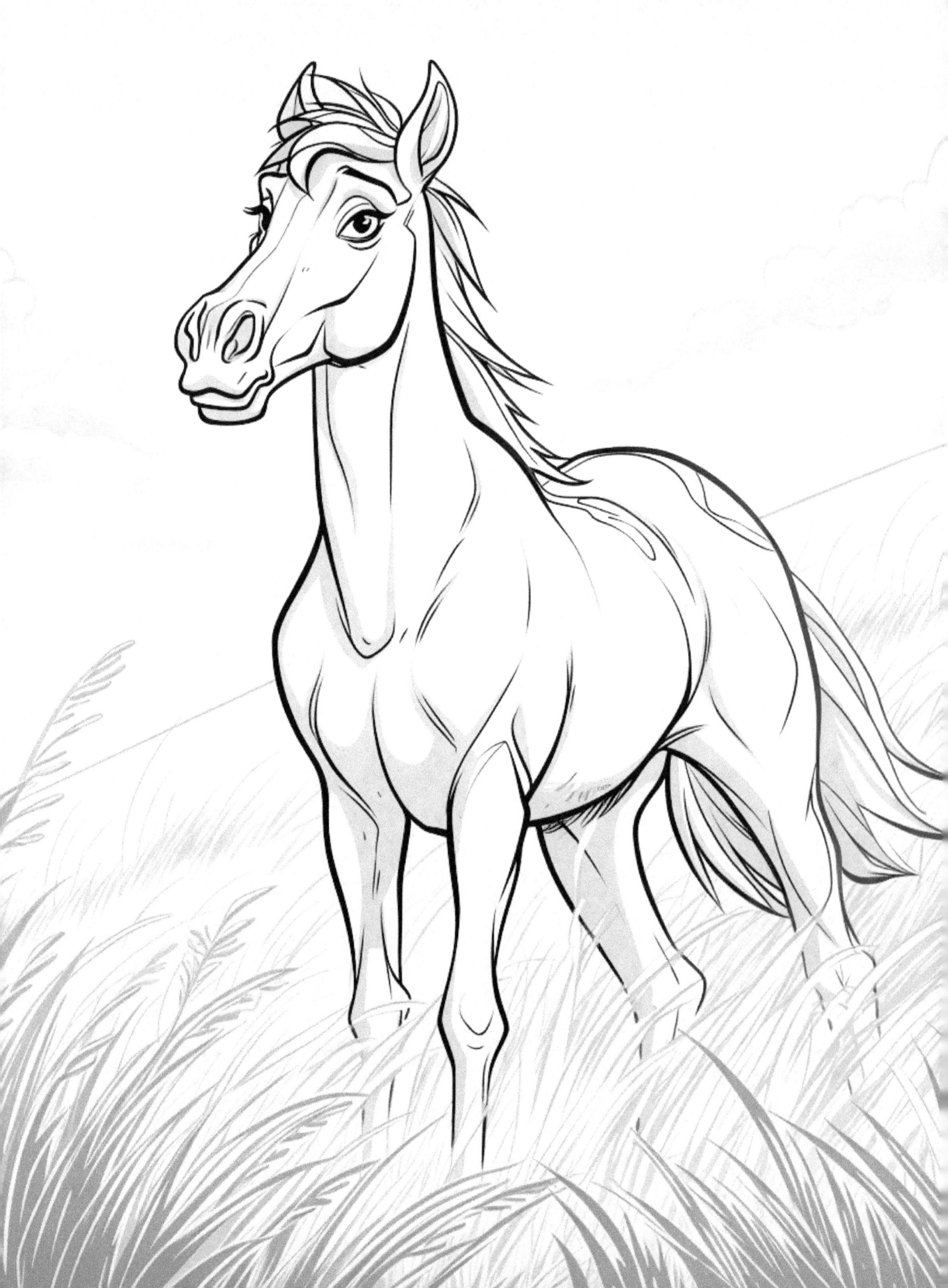

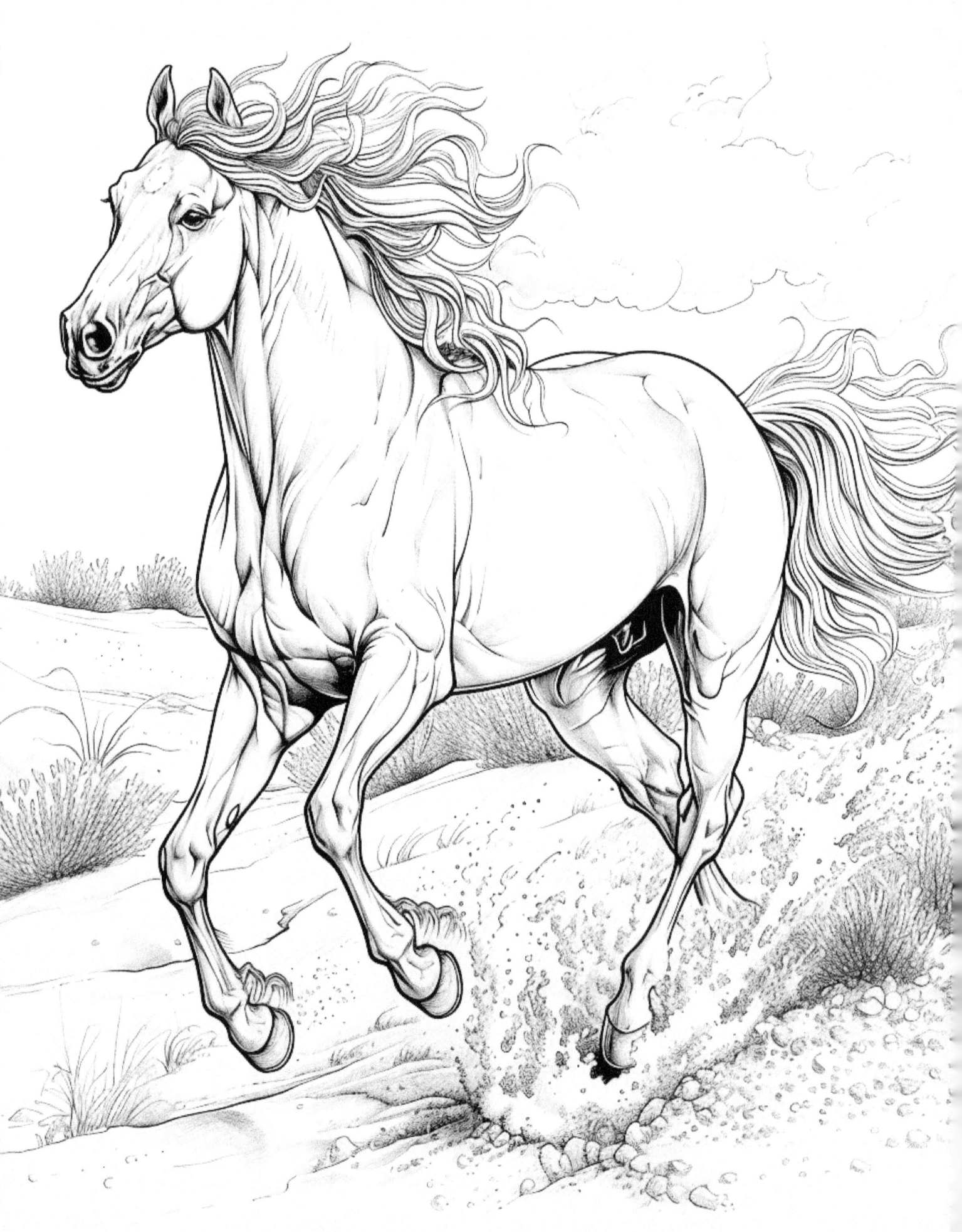

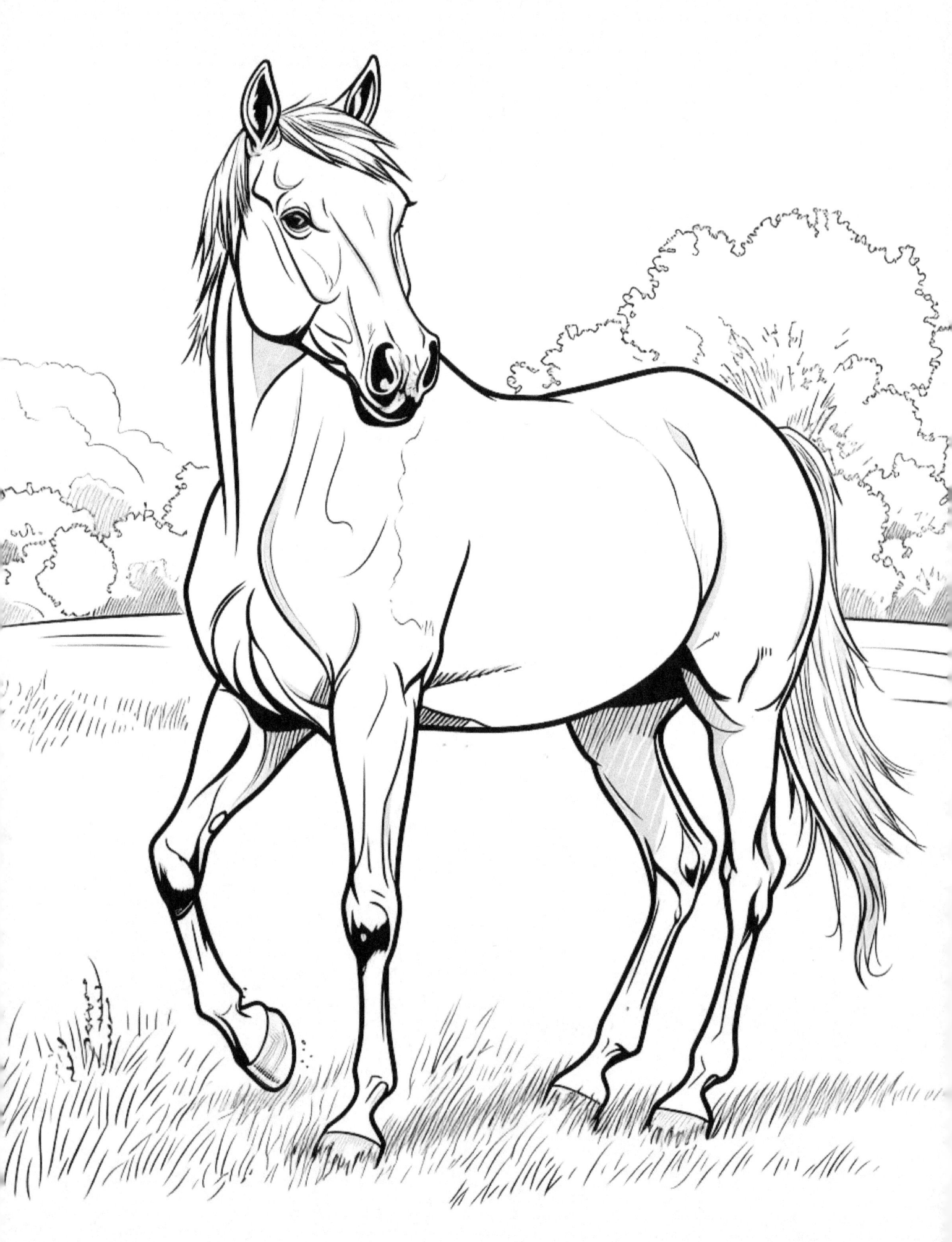

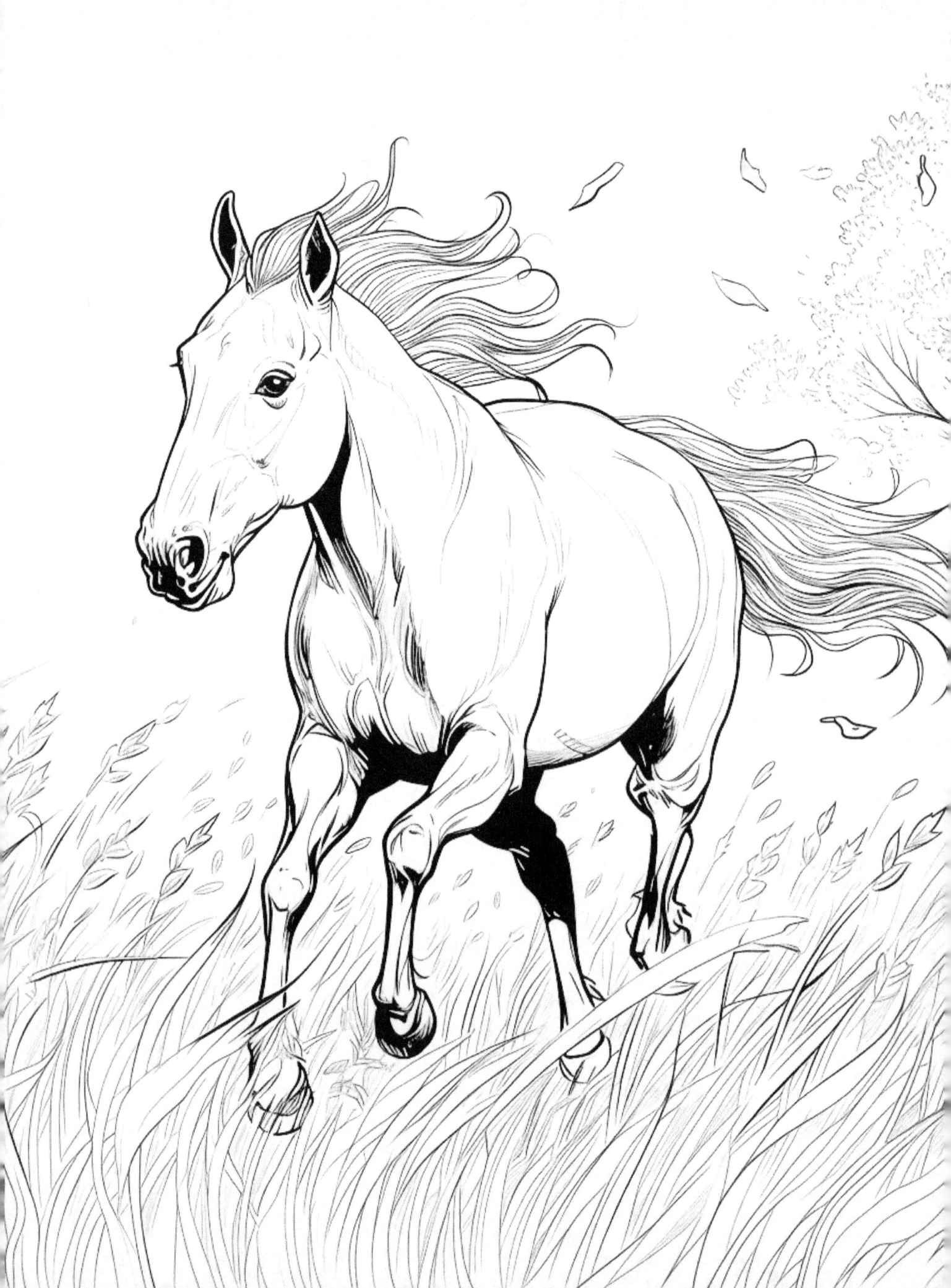

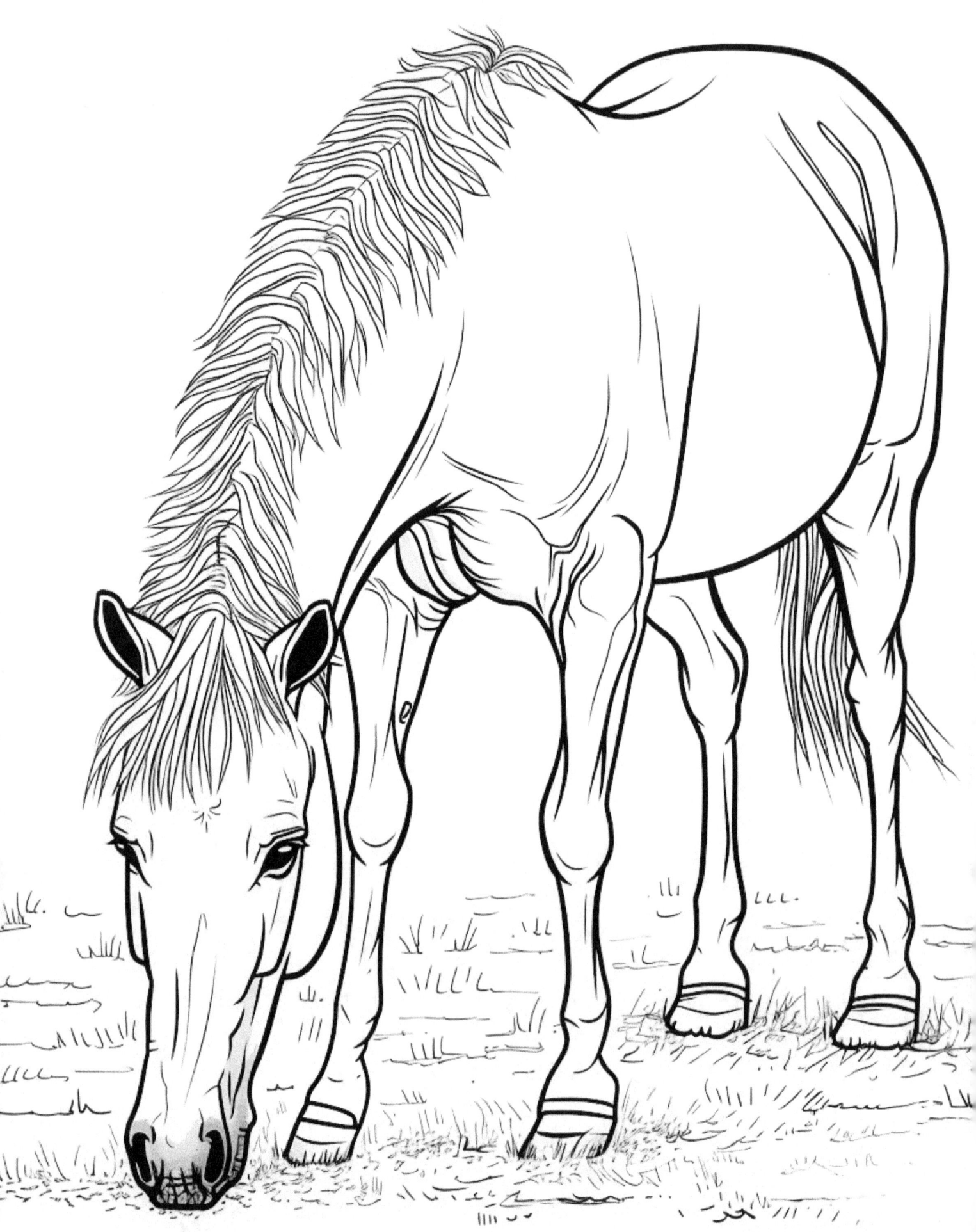

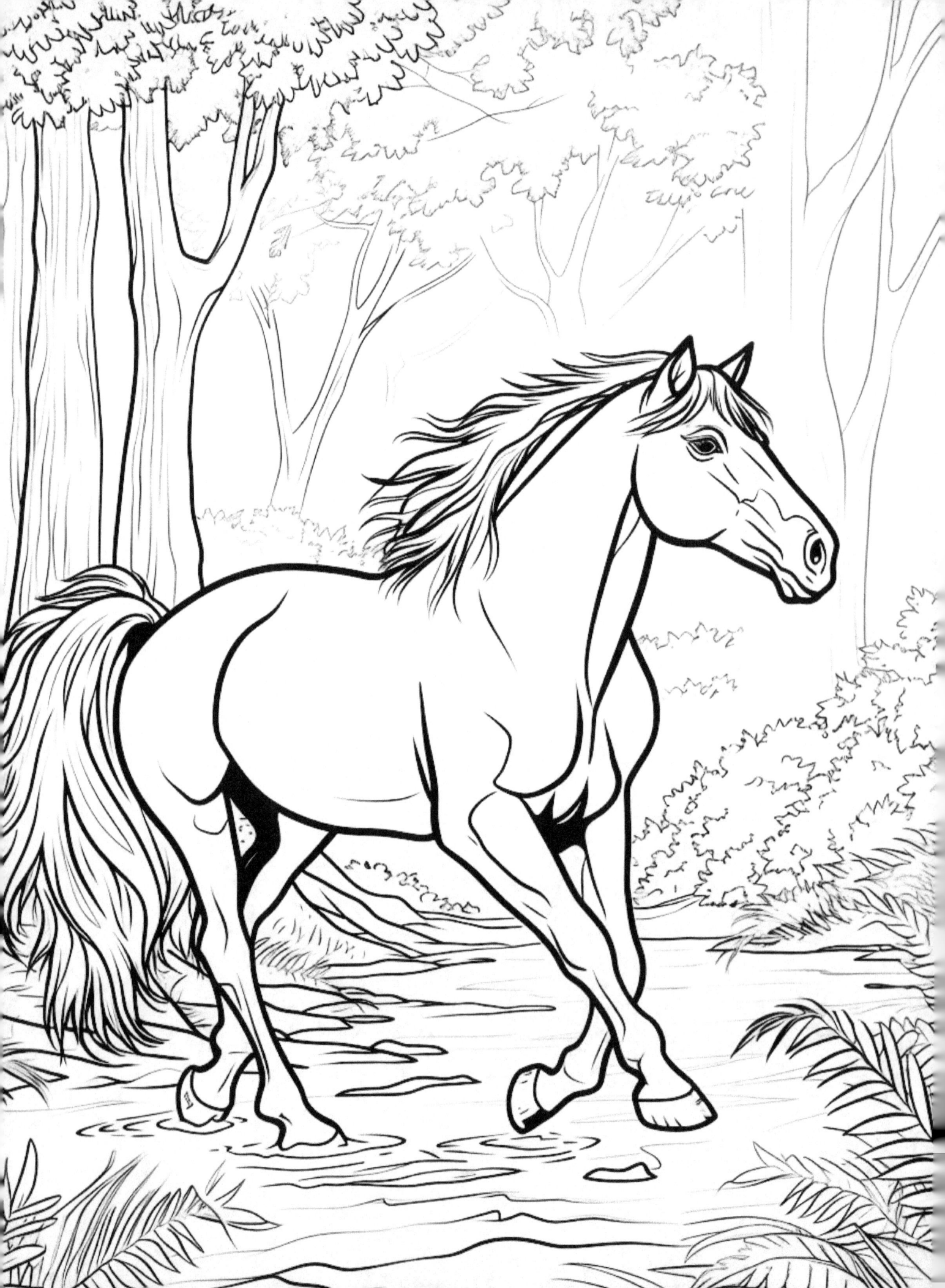

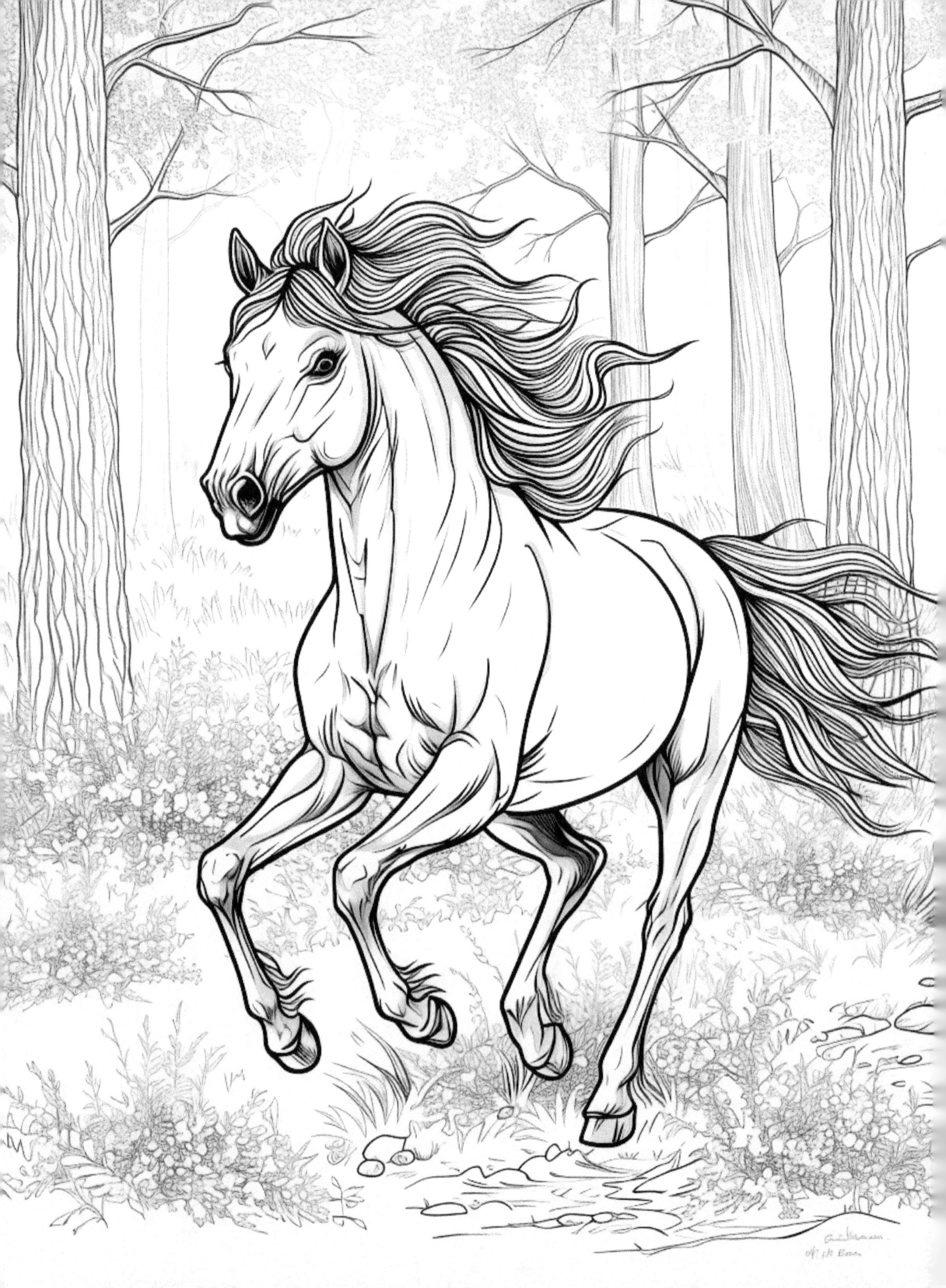

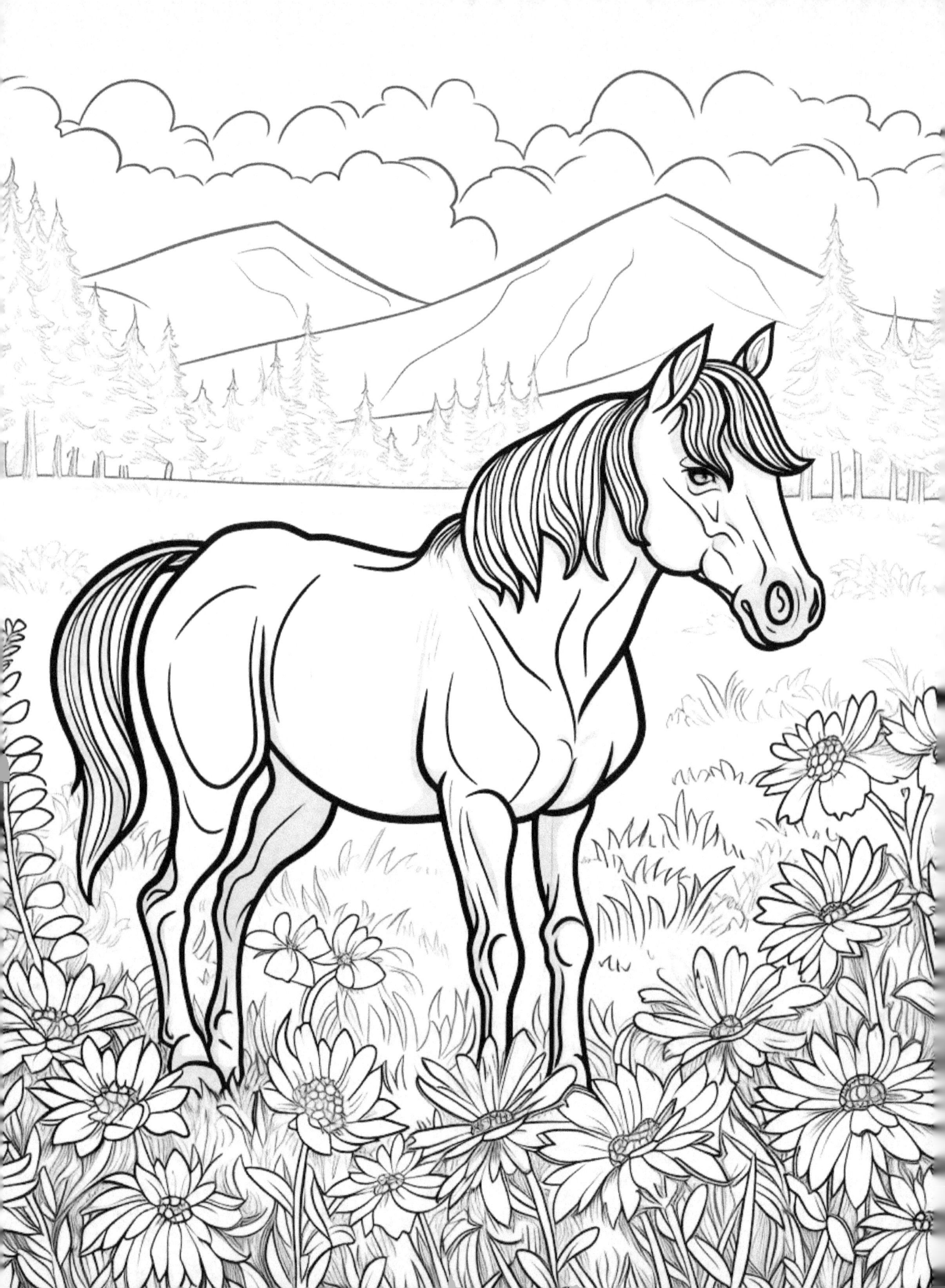

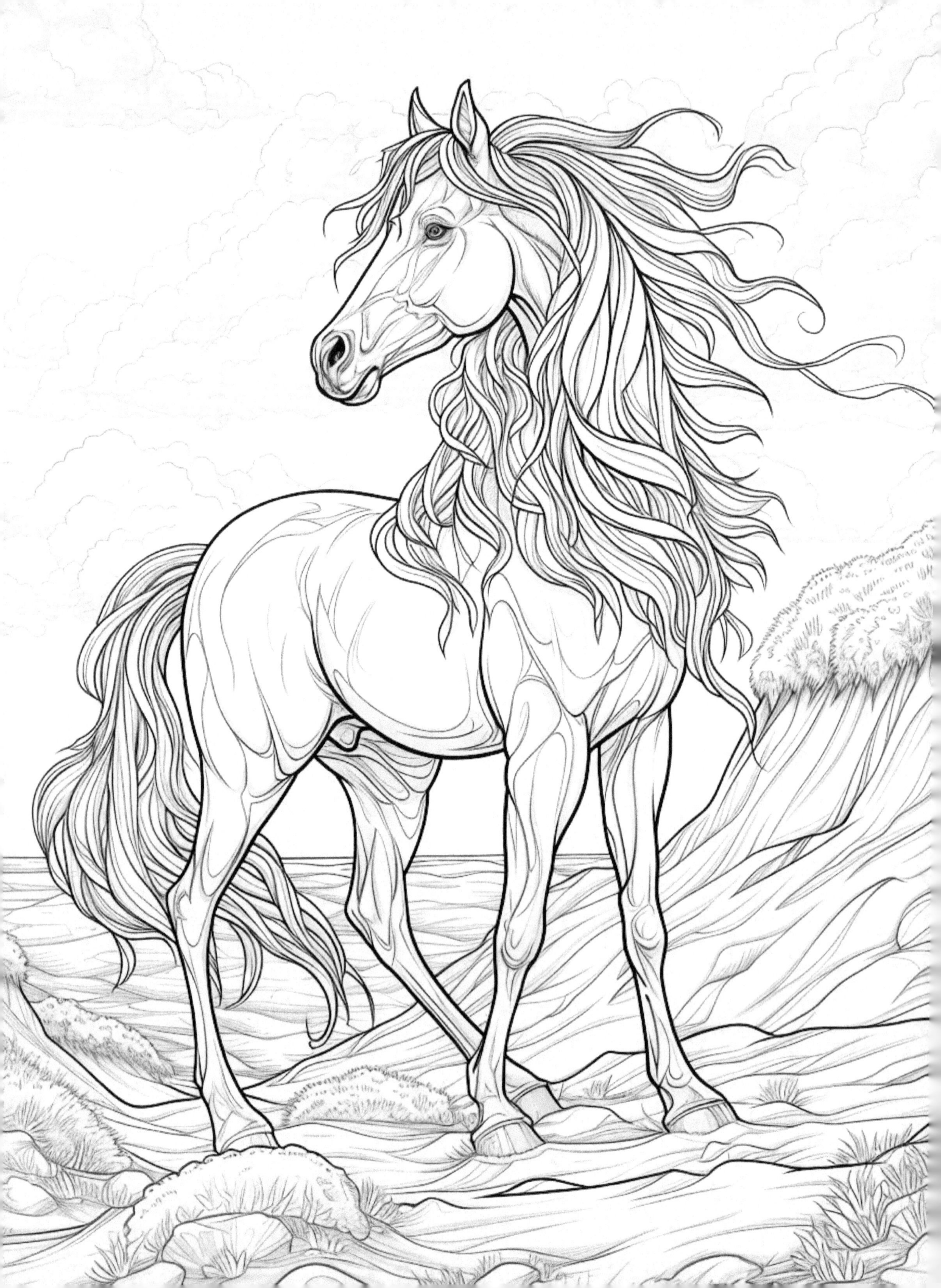

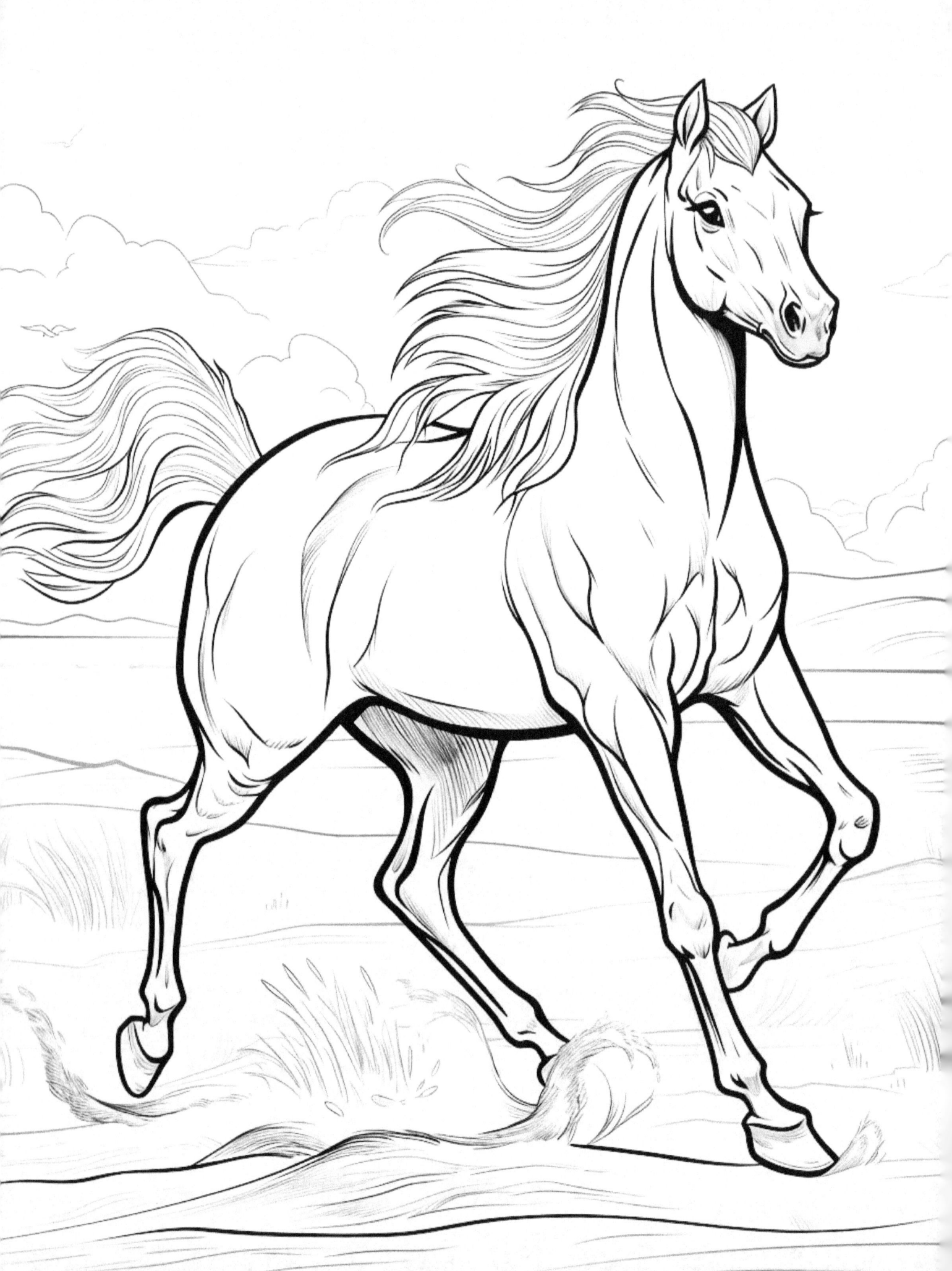

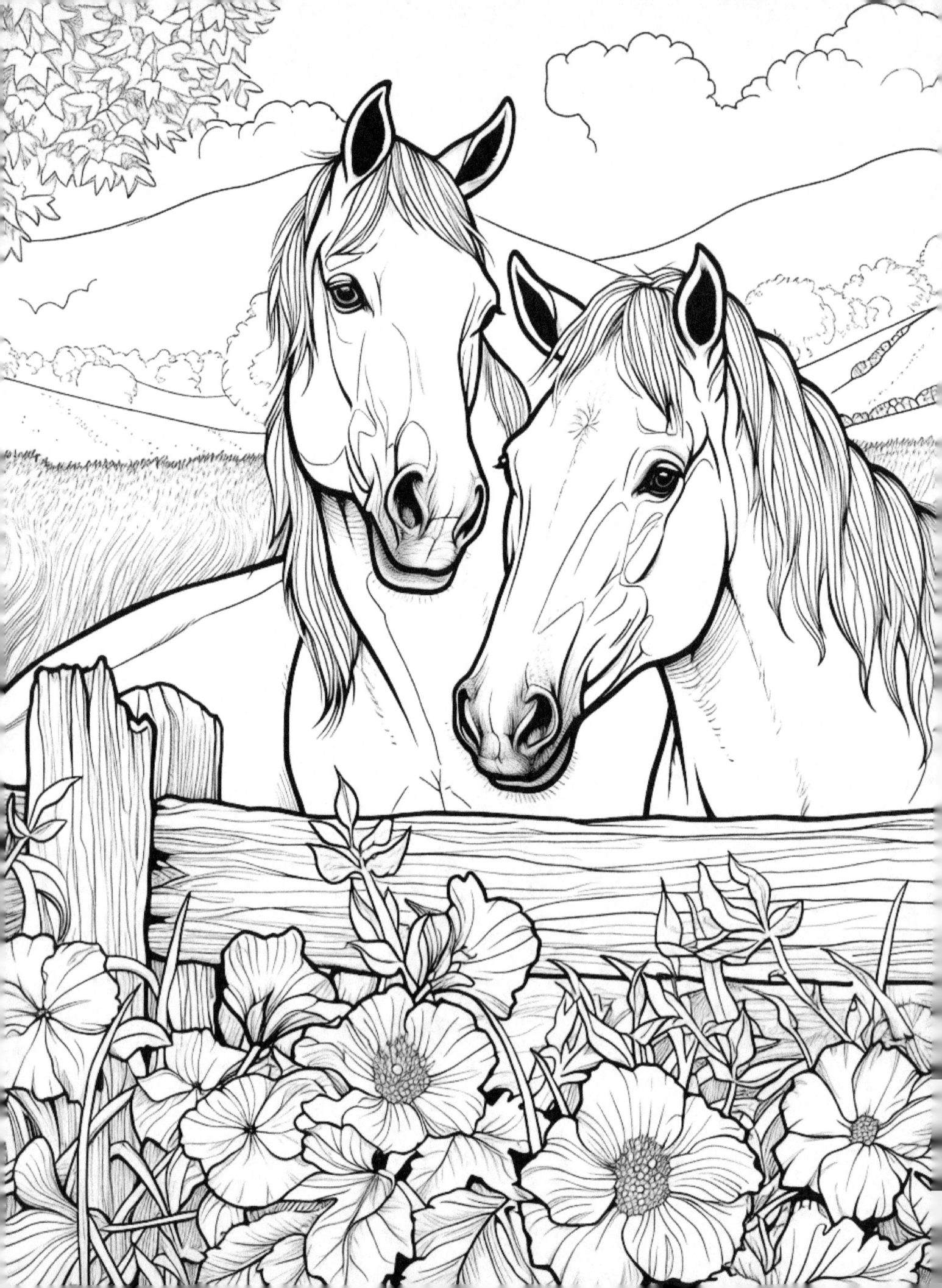

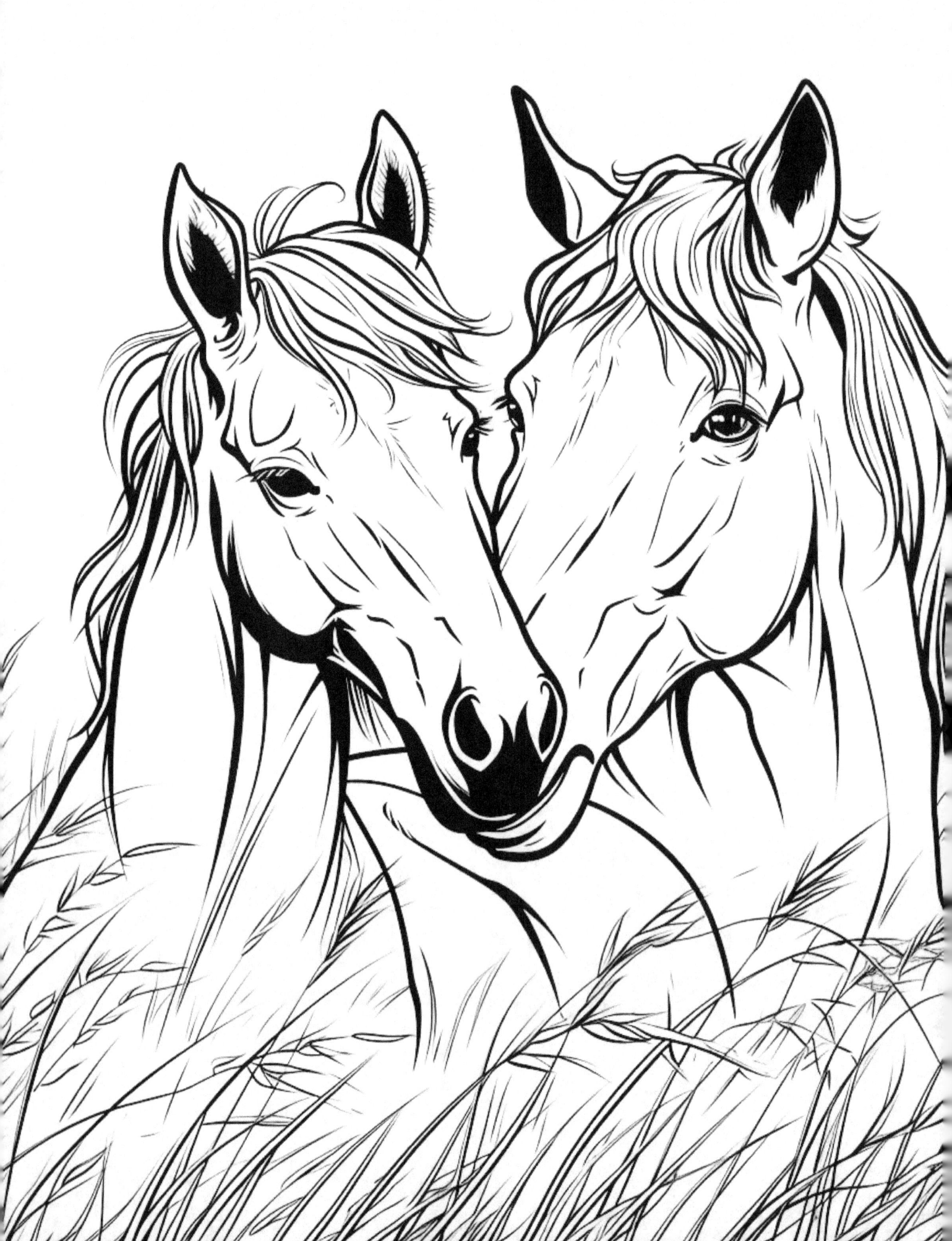

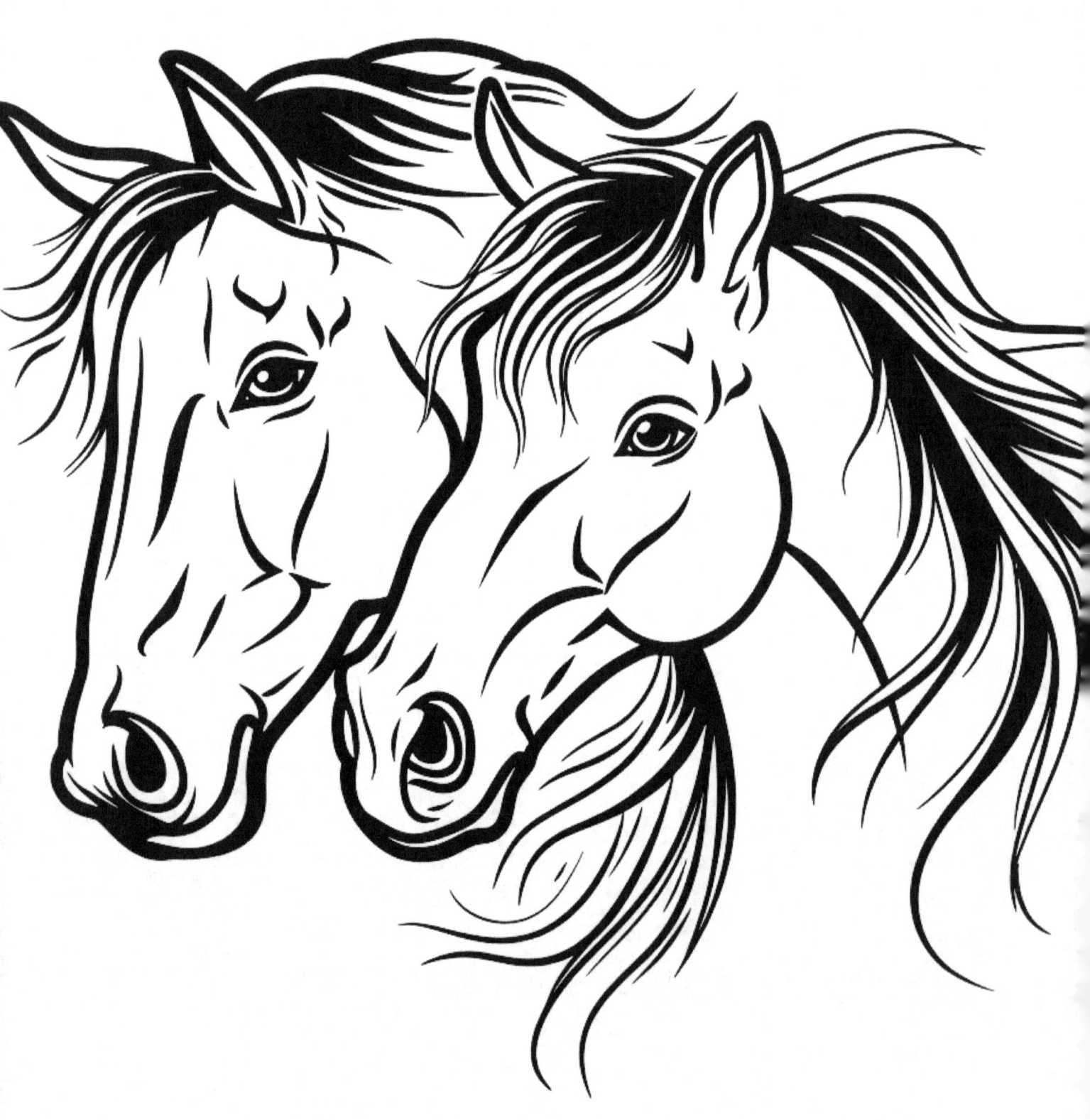

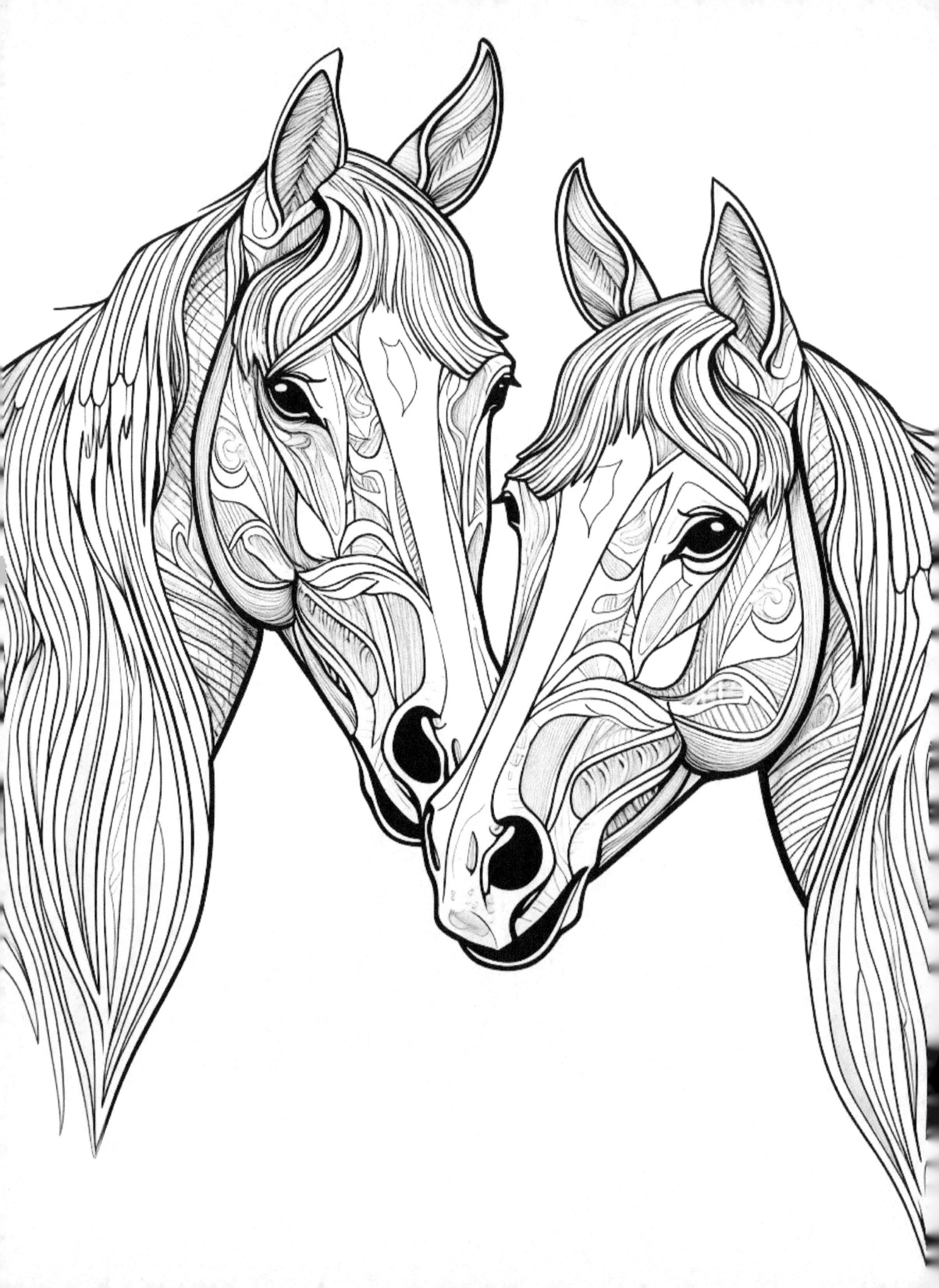

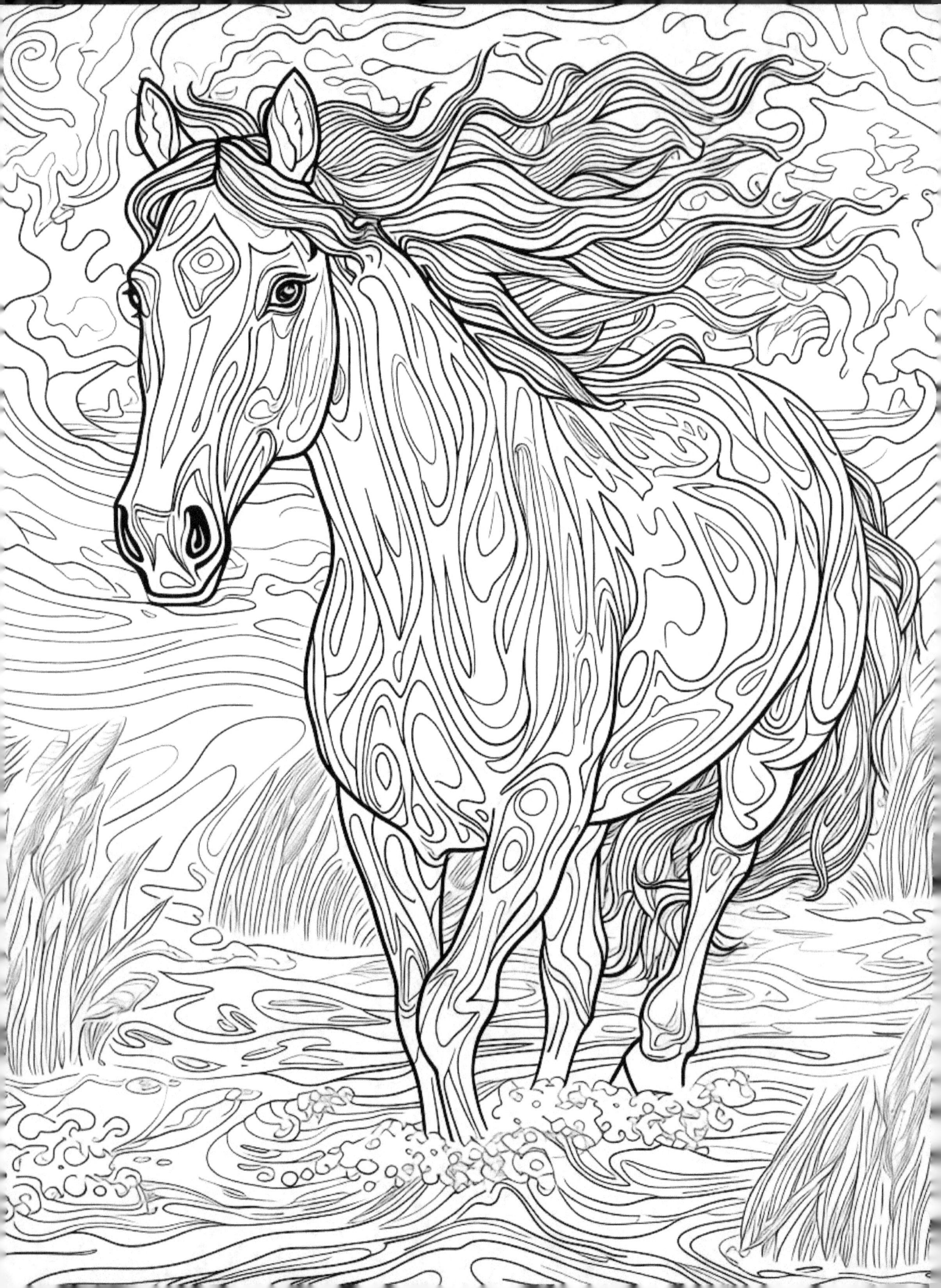

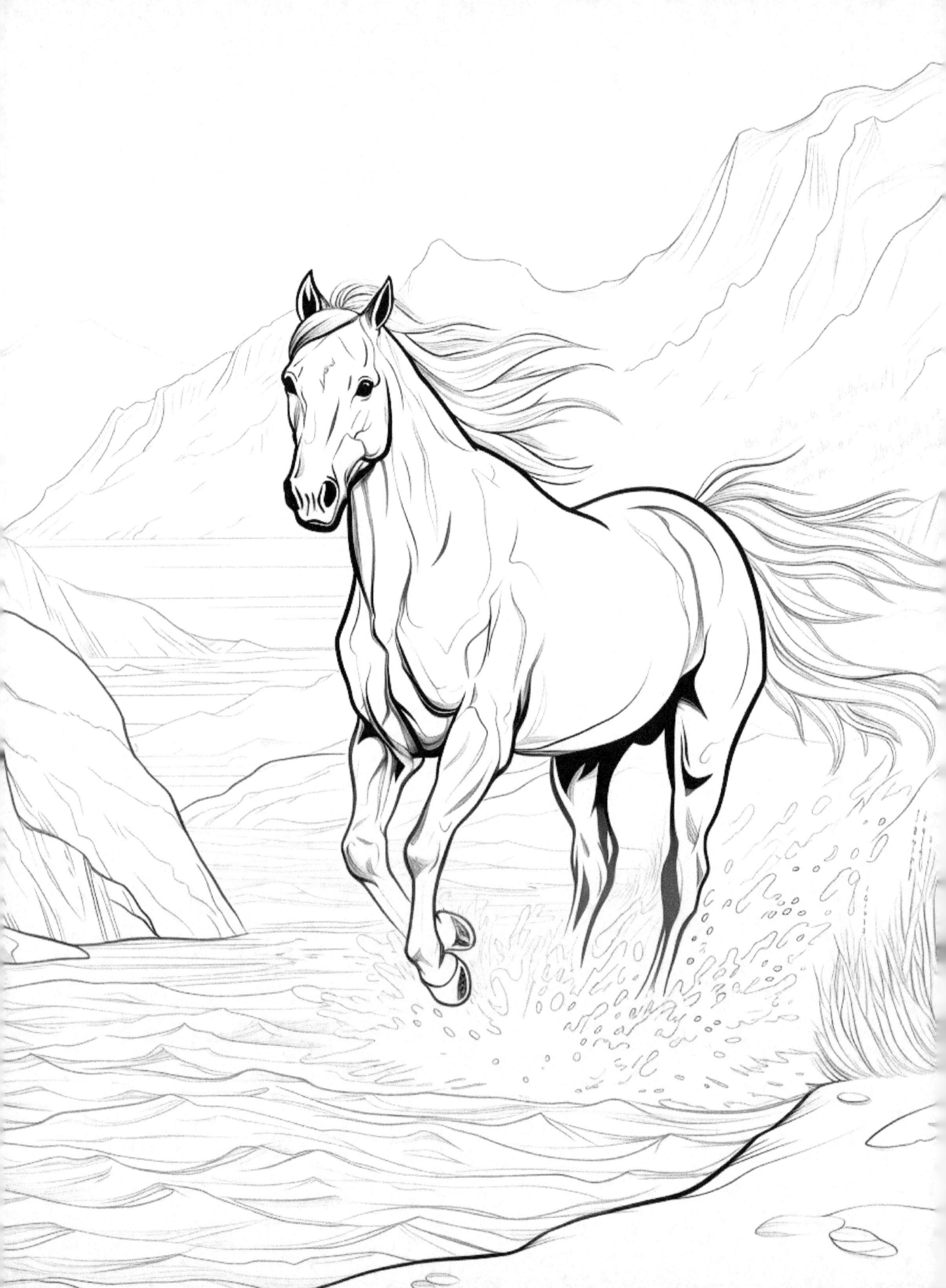

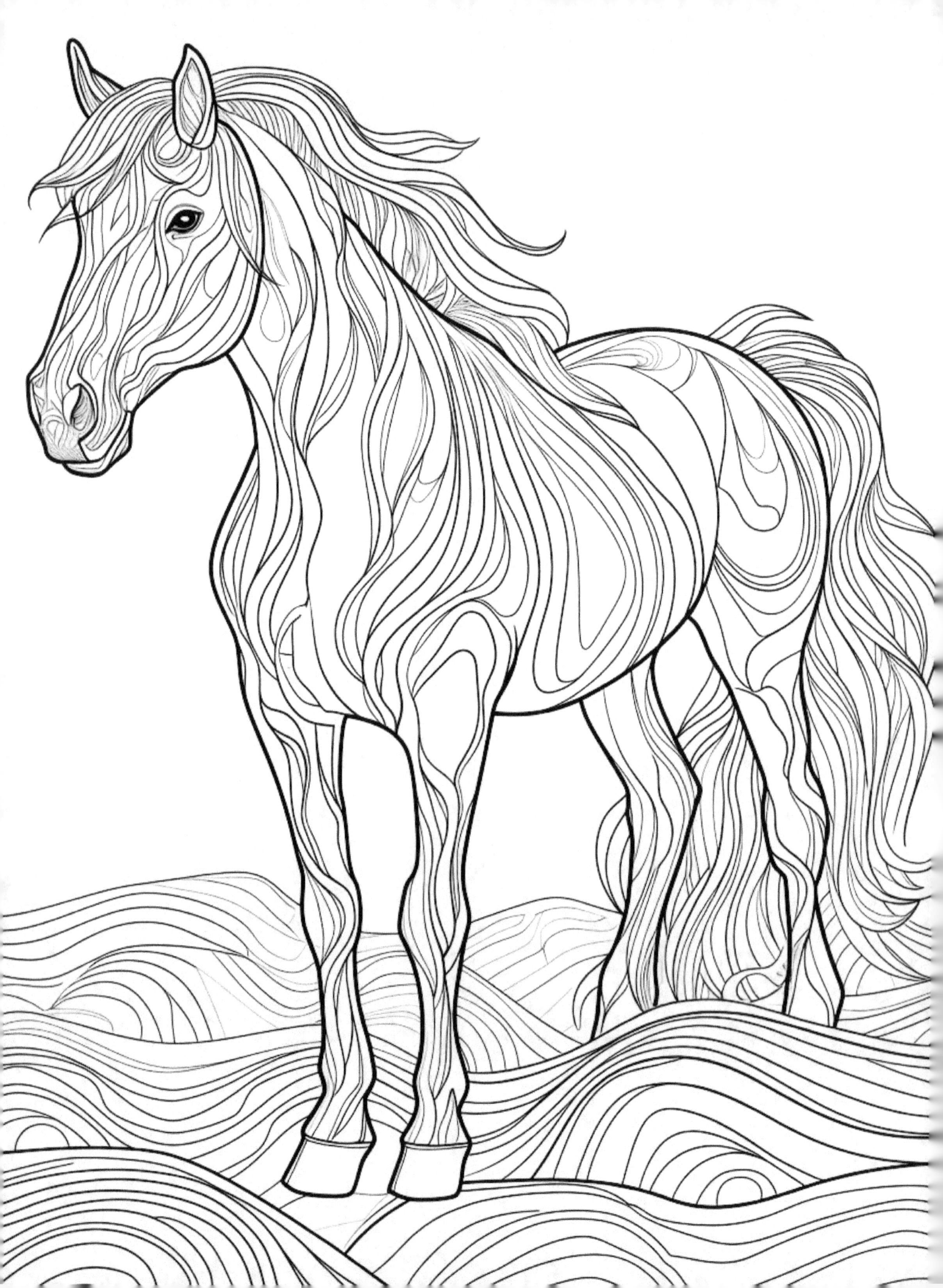

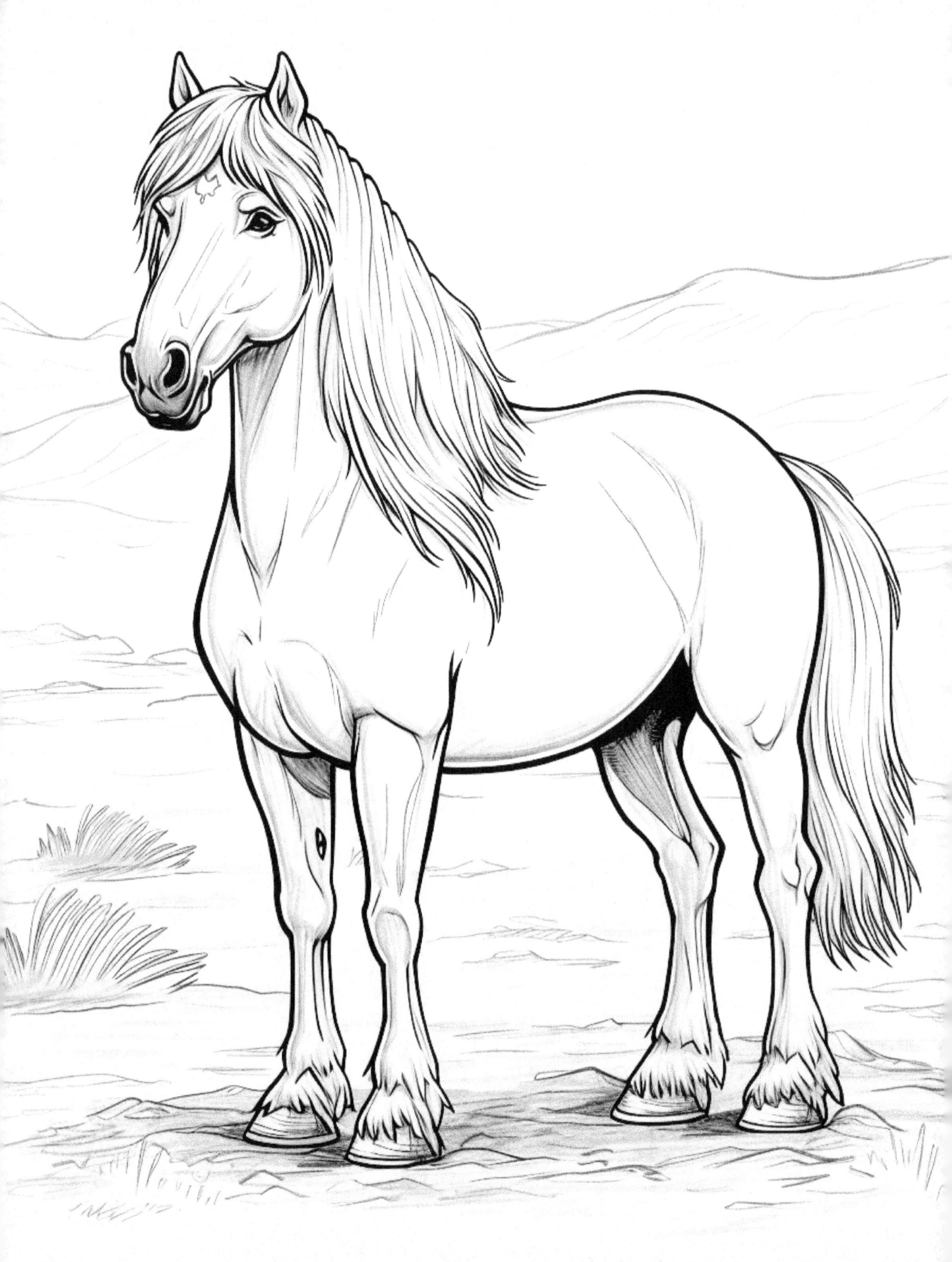

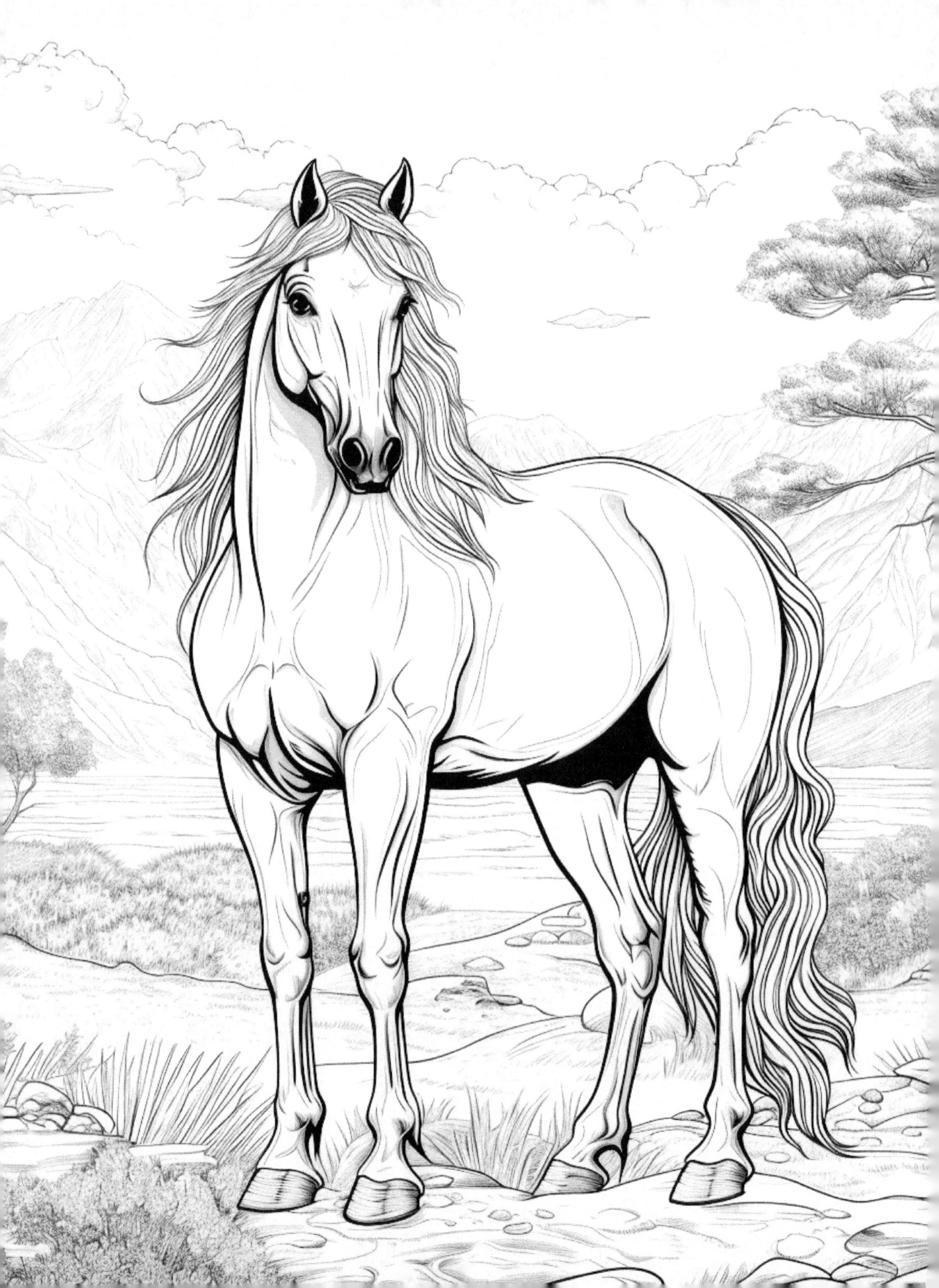

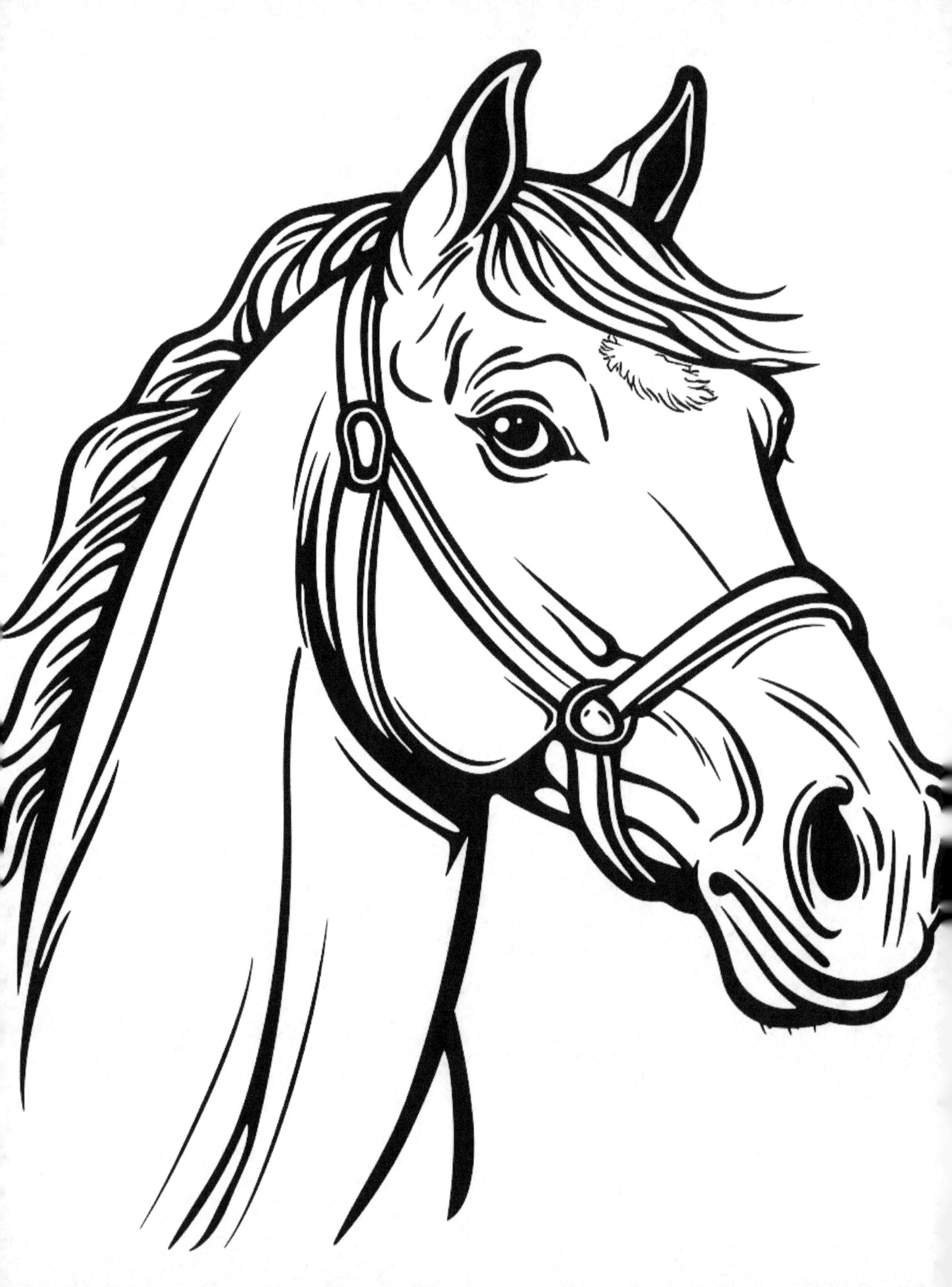

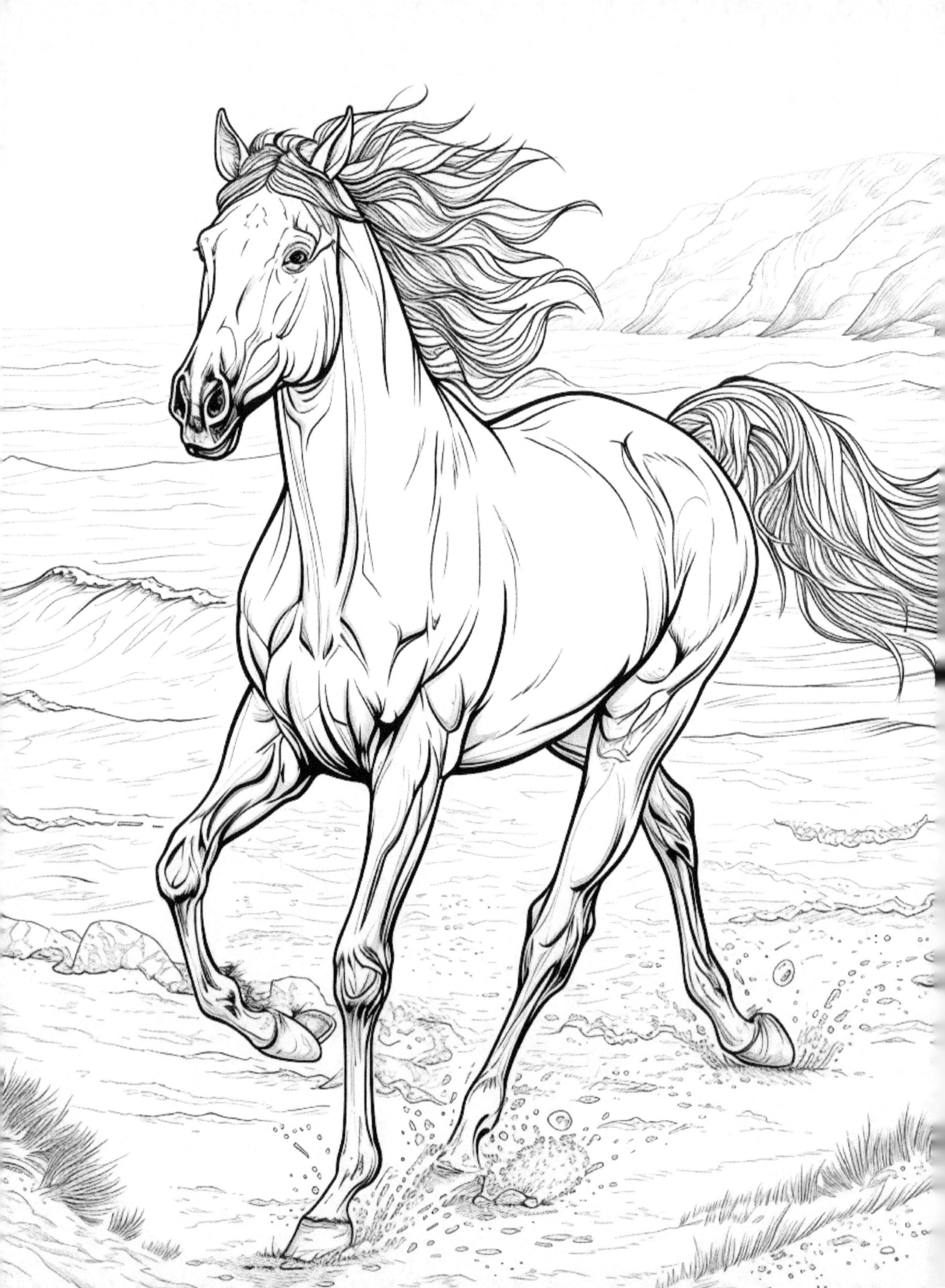

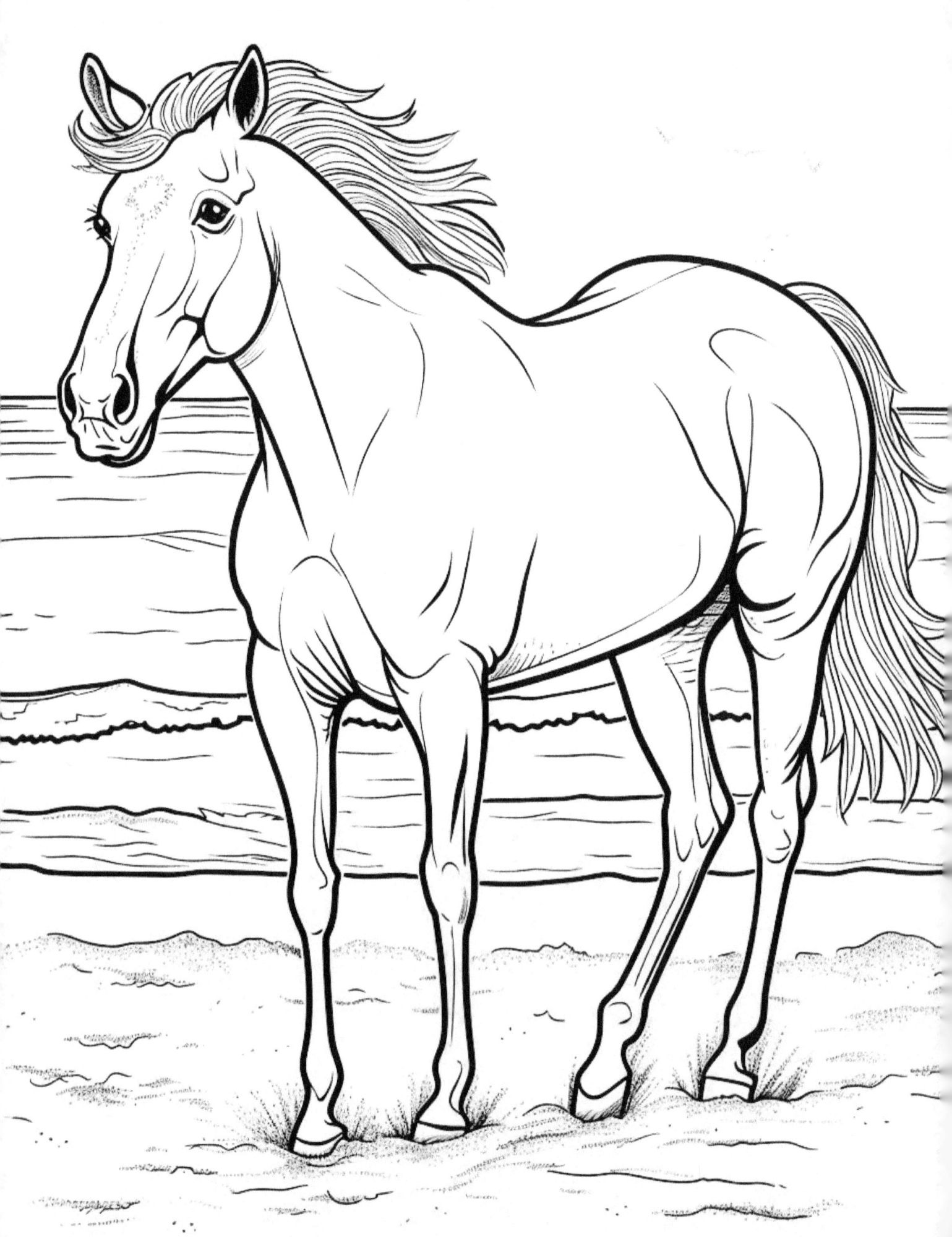

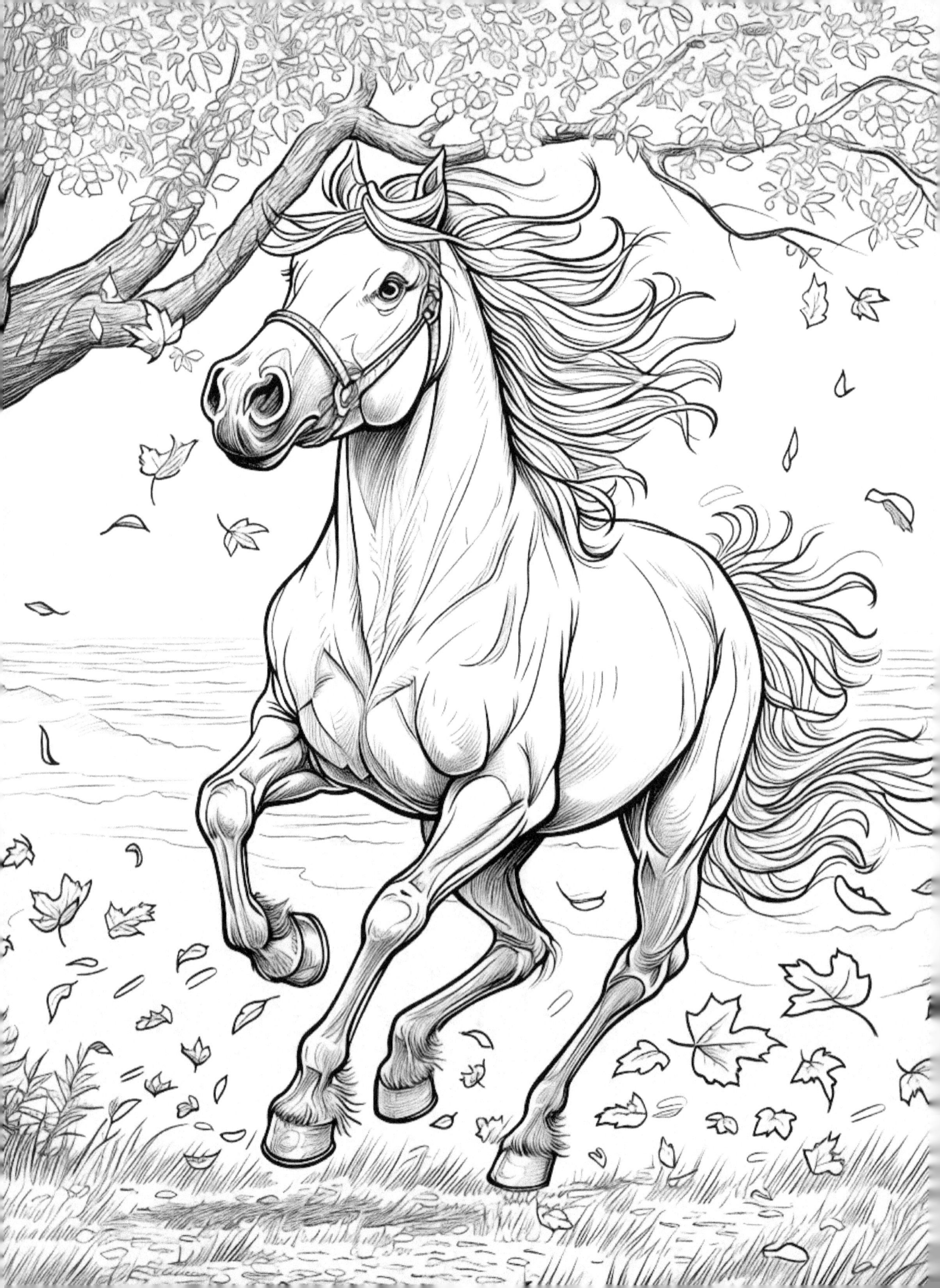

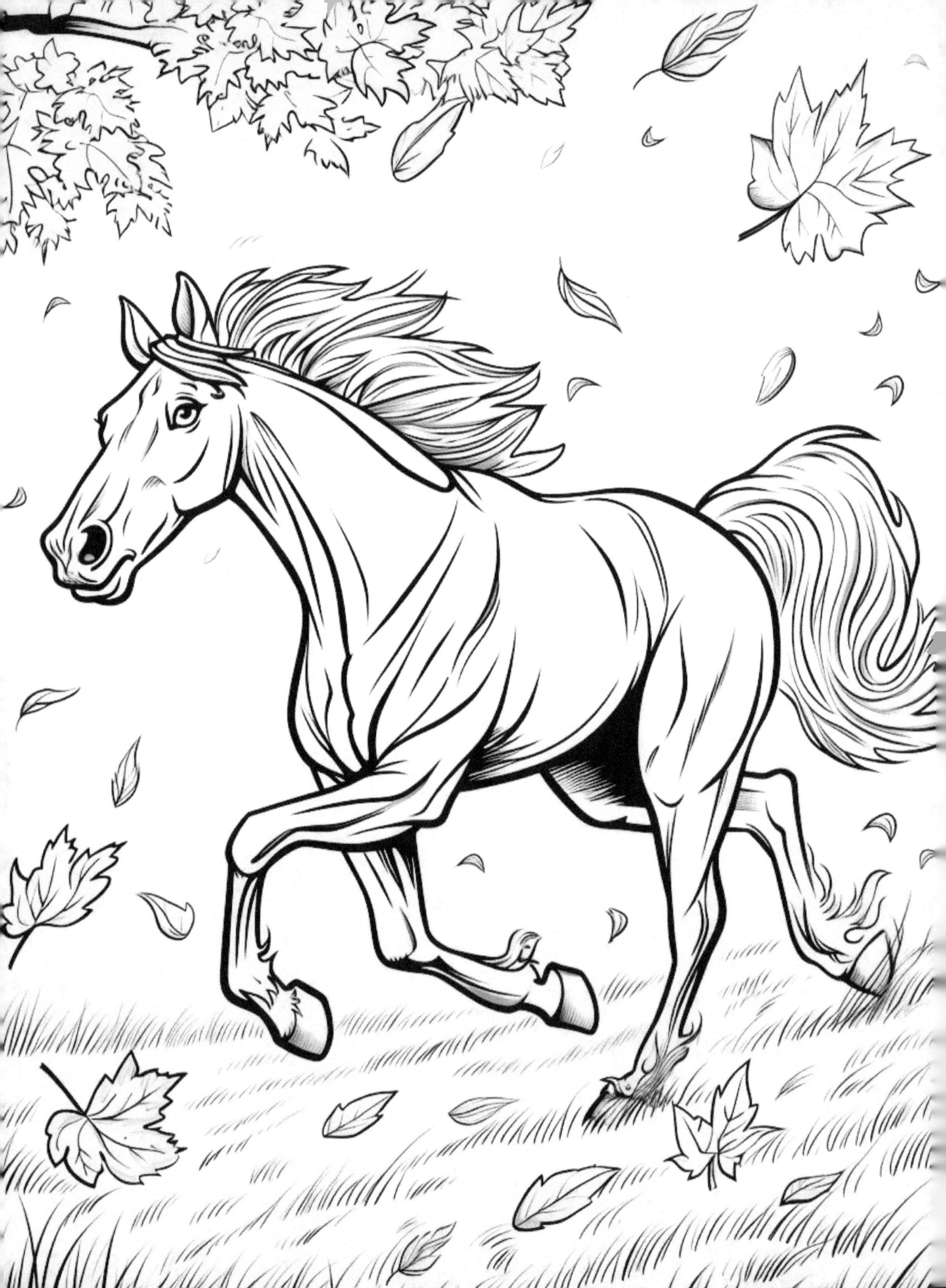

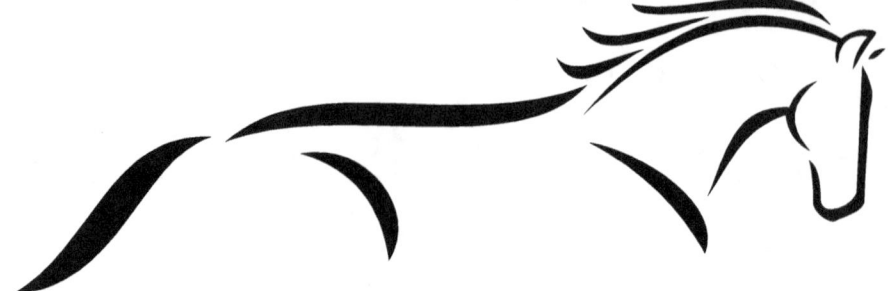

And so your artistic adventure among 67 Majestic Horses comes to an end.

Thank you for joining me in celebrating these noble animals through creativity and relaxation.

May your journey through these pages have brought you moments of joy, wonder and a deeper appreciation of the beauty, strength and spirit of horses.

I hope you will continue discovering new ways to nurture your artistic spirit. Until next time, happy coloring!